The Australian Emigrant a Rambling Story, Containing as Much Fact as Fiction

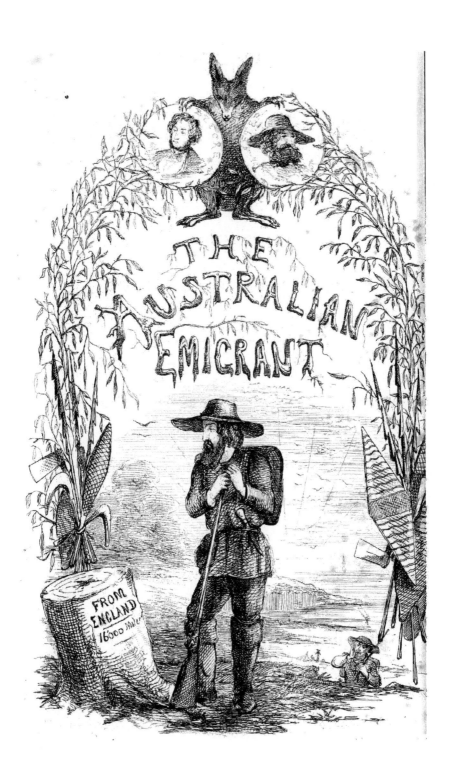

THE AUSTRALIAN EMIGRANT

FROM ENGLAND 16000 Miles

THE

AUSTRALIAN EMIGRANT,

A RAMBLING STORY,

CONTAINING

AS MUCH FACT AS FICTION:

BY G. H. HAYDON,

AUTHOR OF FIVE YEARS EXPERIENCE IN AUSTRALIA FELIX.

WITH

ILLUSTRATIONS BY WATTS PHILLIPS, ESQ.

LONDON:

ARTHUR HALL, VIRTUE, AND CO.

AND W. ROBERTS, EXETER.

1854.

TO

MY FATHER AND MOTHER,

THIS POOR TRIBUTE IS

AFFECTIONATELY INSCRIBED, BY

THE AUTHOR.

PREFACE.

One of the early writers on New South Wales, then better known as Botany Bay, relates an amusing anecdote of a certain colonist, who during a journey in a stage coach, happened to mention that he had lately returned from Sydney. His fellow passengers, who had previously been very agreeable and communicative, became on the instant taciturn, buttoned up their breeches pockets, and shunned any further intercourse with the stranger who was sufficiently hardened to admit a residence in so suspicious a locality. When I state that the substance of the following "rambling story" was gathered in the Bush of Australia, I trust my readers will not consider the example cited above worthy their imitation

The permanent settlement of the part of New Holland with which we have more particularly to deal took place in the year 1835, when Mr. John Batman and a small Company of enterprising Colonists from Van Dieman's Land found on some of the verdant hills about Port Phillip, depasturing ground for their flocks and herds.

The unrivaled position which Australia Felix has attained, lends an almost historical interest to the names of the first settlers, which are here appended :—J. Batman, C. Swanston, J. T. Collicott, J. and W. Robertson, J. T. Gellibrand, M. Connolly, J. Sinclair, T. Bannister, A. Cottrell, H. Arthur, H. Wedge, G. Mercer, and W. G. Sams.

These pioneers endeavoured to establish a right to the land by purchase from the natives, and the following is an exact copy of the original treaty between Mr. Batman, on behalf of the first settlers, " of the one part " and the Aboriginal Native Chiefs of Port Phillip and Geelong " of the other part," for the purchase of certain territory described in the deed.

" KNOW ALL MEN, that we, three brothers, Jaga Jaga, Jaga Jaga, Jaga Jaga, being the principal Chiefs, and also Cooloolook, Bungarie, Yanyan, Moowhip, and Mommarmalar, being the Chiefs of a certain tribe called Dutigallar, situate at and near Port Phillip, called by us, the above mentioned Chiefs, Iramoo and Geelong, being possessed of the tract of land hereinafter mentioned, for and in consideration of twenty pair of blankets, thirty knives, twelve tomahawks, ten looking glasses, twelve pair of scissors, fifty handkerchiefs, twelve red shirts, four flannel jackets, four suits of clothes, and fifty pounds of flour, delivered to us by John Batman, residing in Van Dieman's Land, Esquire, but at present sojourning with us and our tribe, do, for ourselves, our heirs, and successors, give, grant, enfeoff, and confirm unto the said John Batman, his heirs and assigns, all that tract of country situate and being in the bay of Port Phillip, known by the name of Indented Head, but called by us Geelong, extending across from Geelong Harbour, about due south for ten miles, more or less, to the head of Port Phillip, taking in the whole neck or tract of land, containing about one hundred thousand acres, as the same hath been before the execution of these presents delineated and marked out by us, according to the custom of our . tribe, by certain marks made upon the trees growing along the boundaries of the said tract of land, with all advantages belonging thereto unto and to the use of the said John Batman, his heirs and assigns, to the meaning and intent that the said John Batman, his heirs and assigns, may occupy and possess the said tract of land, and place thereon sheep and cattle, yielding and delivering to us, and our heirs and successors, the yearly rent or tribute of fifty pair of blankets, fifty knives, fifty tomahawks, fifty pair of scissors, fifty looking glasses, twenty suits of slops or clothing, and two tons of flour.   In witness whereof we, Jaga Jaga, Jaga Jaga, Jaga Jaga, the three principal chiefs, and also Cooloolook, Bungarie, Yanyan, Moowhip, and Mommarmala, the chiefs of the said tribe, have hereunto affixed our seals to these presents, and have signed the same. Dated according to the Christian Era, this sixth day of June, 1835.

" Signed, sealed, and delivered in the presence of us, the same having been fully and properly interpreted and explained to the said Chief.

	JAGA JAGA,	his x mark
	JAGA JAGA,	his x mark.
	JAGA JAGA,	his x mark.
	COOLOOLOOK,	his x mark.
JOHN BATMAN.	BUNGARIE,	his x mark.
JAMES GUMM.	YANYAN,	his x mark.
WM. TODD.	MOMARMALLAR, his x mark.	

" BE IT REMEMBERED, that on the day and year within written, possession and delivery of the tract of land within mentioned was made by the within named Jaga Jaga, Jaga Jaga, Cooloolook, Bungarie, Yanyan, Momarmalar, and Moowhip, Chiefs of the tribes of natives called Dutigaller and Geelong, to the within named John Batman, by the said Chiefs taking up part of the soil and delivering the same to the said John Batman in the name of the whole.

JAGA JAGA,	his x mark.
JAGA JAGA,	his x mark
JAGA JAGA,	his x mark.
COOLOOLOOK,	his x mark.
BUNGARIE,	his x mark.
YANYAN,	his x mark.
MOOWHIP,	his x mark.
MOMARMALAR,	his x mark.

Signed in the presence of
    JAMES GUMM.
    ALEXANDER THOMPSON.
    WM. TODD."

It is not my intention to enter further upon the History of Port Phillip, my task is of a lighter nature. To those who may be seeking more solid information upon Australian affairs than falls within the scope of a story, a perusal of the various works of John Sidney, particularly his " Hand Book " and " Three Colonies," will completely suffice. The writings of this intelligent author evince such a practical and extensive knowledge of the subjects treated on, that if read with attention, they cannot fail to impress the reader with their worth, nor to impart just and enlightened views upon colonial matters.

Since the first portion of the following pages were in the printer's hands, unavoidable delays have occurred. The arduous duties of a public office must plead as some excuse for errors, which no doubt will be apparent to the critical reader. If I am fortunate enough to amuse some and instruct others, however slightly, my highest hopes will be realized.

LONDON, May, 1854.

AUSTRALIAN EMIGRANT.

CHAPTER I.

SOME dozen years since the desire for emigrating to Australia in preference to America began to be felt and acted upon by the energetic and restless portions of our population, whom nature seems to have designed to become the pioneers of civilization in distant lands. Whilst the greater number of those who left England for our Australian Empire, about the time of which we write, were of the working orders, and travelled as much from necessity as choice; they were accompanied by some who had filled other and better positions, but who, beaten by calamities, disappointments, and reverses, or moved by a speculative spirit, sought in the active employments incidental to a Bushman's life, oblivion of their past failures, or a fresh and promising field for the occupation of their energies. To the colonists, the mechanics and labourers were the most acceptable classes. Their skill and perseverance presented the ready means by which the natural capabilities and the inactive wealth of the country could be brought into operation.

Amongst some to whom Australia Felix, now known as Victoria, presented but moderate elements of success, were those who had passed a sufficient portion of their lives surrounded by the comforts of an English home, to establish habits and induce

B

desires, which are not easily gratified elsewhere. There were
many others, whose qualifications for colonising could scarcely
be considered very promising, and amongst them was the hero
of our story. Without a profession, and having failed in obtaining a cadetship or any other suitable appointment, Hugh
Raymond determined, at the age of twenty-one, to seek in Victoria, for such an opening in life as the land of his birth did
not afford: but before we trace his fortunes further, it is our
purpose to inform the reader, in as brief a manner as possible,
of a few necessary particulars to the elucidation of our story.
Perhaps we shall serve our purpose best by introducing him to
the little party who had assembled on the evening of Hugh's
departure, which consisted of four persons.

Old Mr. Raymond, a retired commander in the British na-
vy, who had been a widower for some years, his two daughters,
and a young lady an attached friend of the family—Hugh included. We take this early opportunity of imparting the fact,
that the attachment was mutual. The young lady, to whom
we have drawn attention, was an orphan, and her guardian was
a lawyer named Jarrol, who resided in the neighbourhood. We
will not hazard the reader's patience, by dwelling too long upon
the occurrences, always more or less painful, attending a parting interview; the indulgent reader's sympathies must supply
the blank we leave.

The breaking day found the family astir.—The old commander's rheumatism was more troublesome than usual—the
girls were looking pale and dejected, and Hugh assumed a
cheerfulness he could scarcely be expected to feel. For a great
part of the night he had been packing, unpacking, and repack-
ing; forgetting and remembering things he should want on the
voyage. He had been trying his hand at sewing in buttons,
and sundry other simple operations of the kind; he had even

gone so far as to form a plan for making a pair of unmention-
ables, and in imagination had built himself a hut from the
flooring to the roof. As feathers show the direction of the
wind, so these trifling matters indicated the presence of quali-
ties requisite to form a successful colonist.

Parting scenes are sacred, and hopes and prayers breathed
at such a season are chronicled elsewhere. Mr. Raymond accompanied his son a short distance on his way to meet the
coach, and, on leaving him, pressed into his hand a bill drawn
on a merchant in Melbourne, as well as some ready cash, bade
" God bless him," and returned with a heavy heart " in all the
silent manliness of grief."

By the evening, Hugh found himself in comfortable quarters at Plymouth, but with a mind disturbed and excited by the
events of the day : he felt, too, not without pride, that he would
now have to look to his own exertions and conduct alone for
independence and success.—

" The wide world was all before him,
But a world without a home "

His dream, that night, was of the happy one he was leaving—
the one he looked for was but as a dream itself.

Any passenger that ever had the ill-fortune to sail in the
" Big Ann," would scarcely have conceived that the most ima-
ginative advertisement could have described her as "a well
known, first class, fast sailing, clipper-built ship; noted for her
great speed, and for her handsome model. her cabins very spacious, and complete with every convenience and comfort." To
the initiated, the " Big Ann " *was* well known—but only as a
" regular tub," that *would* broach-to in foul weather, but could
not make above eight knots an hour under the most favourable
auspices.

Hugh Raymond's only information respecting this vessel was derived from advertisements, and the interested descriptions of her agents. Presuming both to be truthful, he had not hesitated to "secure" an intermediate berth on board, before an opportunity had offered of testing the accuracy of the representations made respecting her. Several mornings after her advertised time of sailing, Hugh, looking from his bedroom window, saw the ominous Blue Peter flying from the mast head of the "Big Ann," indicating that she would weigh anchor in a few hours. Hurrying to the Barbican, he found it already crowded by the free emigrants (very free indeed) going off to the ship in shore boats, the most fortunate of whom could boast, at the best, a bundle dangling at the end of a shillala over the shoulder, whilst the property of the greater proportion appeared to consist of little beyond their positive clothing—if indeed rags deserve such a name. The feeling that he was destined to endure a long voyage in the company of this heterogeneous multitude, most of whom were Irishmen, who were readily to be distinguished by the national weapon they carried, with scarcely an exception, did not tend to raise Hugh's spirits. Many of the poor people appeared to have undergone great privations, and their starved and care-worn countenances told many a sad tale of misery; but even their wretchedness could not obliterate the tenderness and sparkling wit so peculiar to their race.

One poor girl, whilst being assisted into the boat by a tall fellow, cried out in a pitiful voice, "Ohone! ohone! where's the counthry like this, barrin our own?—Where'll we find others like thim in the wide world?" Her full black eyes—for Rose Blaney's eyes were of the blackest, and her face of the prettiest, gazed with a mournful expression on the expanse of water before her. She continued—"Sure the big waves will spare an unprotected girl, and may be, I'll live to come back again wid the gowlden guines, plaze God, and meet the sisters and the brothers I'll lave behind me."

"By the powers but I'll purtect you," said the tall fellow, as he wrapped his freize coat around her, and was about pushing off the boat, when the boatman asked him for his fare.

"Sure, I've got my fair here, and I'll not part wid her," exclaimed "Big Mick," as he was familiarly called by his countrymen, placing his brawny arm round Rose Blaney's waist "to keep her steady," as he said, for the boat was rocking.

"I want sixpence of you," said the boatman.

"Och, murther!" said Mick, "it's sixpence you want of me, is it?—well thin, I've only got four pince, and sure," Mick continued, coaxingly, "you wouldn't take *that*, and lave a poor divil to land in a furrin counthry without a rap."

"Come; none of your blarney," said the boatman; and he repeated his demand for the impossible sixpence.

"Bad scran to ye—ye hard-hearted vagabon—your sowl, if you have any, is as ugly as your face:—now boys," shouted Big Mick, turning about to his countrymen, "will yes make up the other tuppence for me?"

Many hands were immediately thrust into pockets—or rather, pocket-holes, in many cases; but which were quite sound enough for their owners' possessions. Before Hugh had time to carry his impulse into effect and pay the poor emigrant's fare, a handful of coppers were given to Mick. Selecting the required amount, he held it out with the fourpenny piece to the boatman, who was in the act of taking the money, when the Irishman withdrew his hand, and with the most annoying grin in the world said, "Maybe, you'd like to have it all in halfpence—it looks more." Hugh now beckoned Mick to come ashore to him, which he did with the agility of an experienced sailor, and presented him with a shilling, which left the poor fellow in utter confusion at the unexpected increase to his fortune.

Hugh having completed his arrangements with the Agents, received the following note—"To Captain Blomeskull—Ship, 'Big Ann.' Sir, be pleased to shew Mr. Hugh Raymond, who has paid the full amount of an intermediate passage, to the stern cabin below. (Signed,) CRAMMER & HUMM, Agents."

Armed with this missive, and having procured his luggage, Hugh drove to the Barbican, where he underwent the usual attempts at imposition, too palpable even for his inexperience. He succeeded at last in effecting an arrangement with the boatmen, by which those disinterested individuals contracted to carry him, his goods, and his chattels, to the "Big Ann" for *only* double the proper fare, mainly on account of his good looks. The boat was being pushed off, when a young man, whom Hugh had noticed at the Agents' office, ran hastily to the steps from a cab, and finding where the boat was going, desired a passage in her, proffering to pay a share; his request was readily granted, and his luggage being somewhat scanty, was soon disposed of, and he leaped lightly into the boat. Several drunken sailors made similar applications. Hugh, however, declined this inconvenient addition to his cargo, and pushing into deep water, received a volley of imprecations in return— none of your mincing, doubtful, half-joke, half-earnest curses, but such round oaths as only enter into a drunken sailor's or a sober convict's heart to conceive, and are uttered from no other lips with half the appearance of sincerity.

"I see," said the last arrival, after finishing a survey of Hugh's luggage, "you sail in the 'Big Ann,' so do I. She looks a fine craft as far as paint will make her, but from all I hear, she don't act up to her looks, and she's got a rough lot aboard her.—Intermediate, I see, Sir," continued this commu-

nicative gentleman, "so am I: my name, Sir, is Slinger—
Walter Slinger. I've abjured cards, so can't present you with
one; but you will allow me to substitute *this*," and he held
before Hugh's eyes the haft of a large pocket knife, on the silver mounting of which his name appeared. To complete the
introduction (for Hugh was rather pleased than otherwise with
the eccentric Mr. Slinger), he directed that gentleman's attention to the name on one of his chests.—"I am happy to make
your acquaintance, Mr. Hugh Raymond," said Slinger, as he
read the address on the box: "let me hope that our novel
acquaintance may, during the long voyage we are about to un-
dergo, ripen into friendship." Mr. Slinger became very confidential, and o'er the "Big Ann" was reached, had delivered
himself of a brief history of his past life, his present condition,
and future prospects; all which information was, in a great
measure, lost on Hugh, whose mind wandered back to his recent parting with all those he loved so well.

"Here we are," said the boatmen, as they ran under the
stern of the "Big Ann." Several boats were alongside with
steerage passengers, who were scrambling up, and making no
slight discord in their clumsy attempts at getting aboard ship.
The bulwark of the vessel was thronged with men, women, and
children, all examining the new comers with an interest that
already indicated the énnui of a long voyage. "Big Mick"
towered above the mass, and had evidently not yet thought it
prudent to relinquish his post of protector to his pretty little
countrywoman, whom he took under his wing in the morning,
not that Rose Blaney could be seen from the boat, but Mick's
attentions, which were of no ordinary kind, were evidently addressed to somebody of low stature and in an unmistakeable
manner: there was something about the twinkling of his eye,
and the turn of his head, and the position of his arm still occu-

pied in keeping somebody "steady," which left no shadow of a doubt, in Hugh's mind, that Rose Blaney's pretty face would be one of the first to welcome him; and so it was, for as Hugh was clumsily mounting the side, a brawny arm met him part way, and Hugh felt himself lifted on board with very little further exertion on his part.—"God save you," said Mick."—"God save us all," said the little Irishwoman: and this was Hugh's first introduction upon the deck of an emigrant ship.

As soon as Hugh had time to look around, the first object which attracted his attention was an officer of the ship standing with a number of stout bludgeons under his arm, which every now and again was increased by the addition of others. When the bundle became inconveniently large, a rope-yarn was called for and they were tied tightly together. Then the mate mounting upon a beef-barrel, which was at hand, addressed the steerage passengers,—"Now you see, my boys, I'm an Irishman myself (though, for an Irishman, he certainly had a peculiarly Devonian accent), and I know that the most inconvenient thing any countryman of mine can take to sea with him is his shillala; I have therefore, for your own peace and for the general peace of the ship, thought it best to collect all the sticks—steward, give the boys a lot of liquor round—every mother's son of 'em (cheers from all quarters)—as I was saying then, boys, about the sticks and the liquor, the best thing is to stick to the liquor, and to the devil with the sticks; saying which, the mate, with a hearty good will, cast the bundle into the sea; they sunk immediately, for they were of solid blackthorn. A murmur of disapprobation arose at the summary proceeding, which, however, was cut short by the appearance of the ship's steward with a can of rum.

Hugh was now joined by Slinger and the mate, who introducing himself as Mr. Moriarty, requested the pleasure of a glass of wine with his passengers. They accepted the invitation, and presented their notes (for Slinger had received a similar one to Hugh's). The mate after reading them, said, "Well, gentlemen, we have several more passengers than we anticipated," (emigrant ships generally have,) "and the cabin to which I am directed to show you contains nine berths; but I hope you will be all very comfortable."

Mr. Slinger whistled the air "Hope told a flattering tale"—he said nothing; but both our friends felt somewhat uneasy at the idea of nine persons sleeping in a cabin which the mate further informed them was about 13 feet by 9. After a short time the mate proposed showing them their berths; and after taking them through a long dingy portion of the ship, with cabin doors on one side, a narrow locker which ran the whole length in the middle, and a half-inch partition on the opposite side, dividing the steerage passengers from the "intermediates," led them into a still darker and more dismal looking place, which bore the ominous and appropriate name of "the stern cabin below." Both Hugh and Slinger, although they thought they had prepared themselves for the worst, were somewhat surprised at the appearance of the cabin. Hugh could not help referring to a copy of the advertisement, setting forth all the comforts of the "Big Ann:"—"Containing every accommodation," muttered Hugh. "And so it does," said the mate, evidently determined to make the best of matters.—"Look here! here's two bull's eyes, a port hole which can be opened in fine weather, a looking-glass for shaving, snug bunks, and, in fact," continued he, glancing his eye round the cabin, "there *is* every accommodation."

After their eyes had become accustomed to the light, or rather, want of it, they could vaguely distinguish a row of what had much the appearance of four deal coffins without covers placed close together, about two feet above four similar pieces

C

of wood-work, a few inches from the floor. These were the
"snug berths," and were all fixed athwart ship; one only (the
ninth) being placed fore and aft. They were so "snug," that
if Smith happened to fall sick, and such disagreeables *do* happen
at sea occasionally, Jones would be a sufferer as well; and if
Jones, turning round in his bunk, should tickle Brown's nose
with the tassel of his night-cap, and Brown, thus startled, and
throwing his arms abroad should find one of his fingers seized
between Robinson's teeth, certain explanations would be need-
ed, and the "snug" cabin would be in an uproar.

Slinger was advised by the steward to take the fore-and-aft
berth, which was unoccupied, and he chalked his name on the
side in conspicuous characters, feeling, whilst doing so, as if he
were writing an inscription upon his own coffin. Hugh, in
the mean time, had taken formal possession of one of the bunks,
and to put his right beyond doubt, was stretched in it full
length, enjoying the luxury of a pipe

Hugh groped his way upon deck just in time to witness
the arrival on board of a very stout, over-dressed, coarse-
looking personage, who was accompanied by his wife, a fe-
minine edition of her lord: he was superintending the recep-
tion of his luggage from a large flat-bottomed boat crowded
with huge boxes and deal cases. "Get up the pianner first,"
he said, pointing to an oblong case of considerable dimensions,
"and then all the furniter."—"That keg contains ammunition,
put it as far away from my cabing as possible, will you, mate?"
he said, to Mr. Moriarty who was at hand; "and just see them
eight boxes put in my place, will you?" which directions were
all given with great pomposity of manner.

"Your cabin," said the mate, in a respectful tone, will not
contain one half of that luggage: the regulations of the ship do
not permit passengers to usurp the place of her officers either, Sir."

"Who are you, Sir?" said this would-be-important personage.

"Mr. Moriarty, the first mate of the 'Big Ann,' and your humble servant, Sir," said the mate with a bow. "You, I presume, Sir, are a passenger, and your name is ———," and the mate paused for a reply, which the stout person did not make, but looked at his questioner from head to foot, and then from foot to head, then sideways, and at length finishing by walking round him, evidently bent on annihilating him on the spot. But the emigrant officer was made of sterner stuff; it required something more than an insolent stare to put him off his duty. The nameless gentleman (?) commanded one of the men to put the eight boxes into his cabin. The seaman demurred, and requested to know from a brother ar, "how long old Forty Stun had been chief officer?"

Mr. Moriarty hereupon delivered *his* commands—"Lower this gentleman's merchandise into the hold, my lads: leave him four out of the eight boxes, and that is one more than he can stow in his cabin."

The important passenger grew purple with rage as this order was being obeyed:—he was speechless for some time; but at last advancing to the mate, who looked him full in the face, he burst out—"Do you know who I am, Sir?"

"How should I, Sir? you have declined telling me," said the mate, with an imperturbable countenance, and a nonchalance which indicated that he had no great curiosity to know.

"I am a cabin passenger," he exclaimed.—

"We have thirty others, Sir," said the mate. This interruption was not heeded by the stout gentleman.—

"I am a Colonial Official, Sir-r-r," he hissed out.—

"I am happy to inform you," replied the collected mate, "that I believe you to be the only one of that kind on board." —Not heeding the interruption, the passenger continued.—

" 1 am a gentleman, Sir: my appointments are numerous."

"And no doubt, profitable," interrupted the mate, eyeing the quantity of gold ornaments ostentatiously displayed on the persons of his new acquisitions.

The fat man could command himself no longer: he burst into a violent fit of swearing, and threatened the mate, that if he had him in the colonies six dozen should be his reward.

The mate smiled at the successful manner in which he had "trotted out" the Colonial Magistrate, and turning upon his heel, left him to dispose of the four remaining boxes (all the rest of his luggage had been lowered into the hold,) as he pleased.

"That's the way we treat these colonial aristocrats," said the mate to Hugh.

After this scene, Hugh retired to his cabin, and for lack of a better seat, perched himself upon his berth, and waited with some anxiety to see who his *compagnons de voyage* were to be.

A party of four, who had previously been on board, soon made their appearance, wished Hugh a good day, deposited sundry articles of bedding in their berths, and again retired. An old captain in the army then introduced himself to Hugh, explained to him he had lately sold out, that he had his family with him on board, but as the cabin he had taken was too small to accommodate all of them, he was content to make one of the nine. Two brothers, who, having no choice, were obliged to take the remaining berths on the ground tier, completed the number; and thus the superior cabin, 13 feet by 9, had its complement.

On the evening of the next day, the decks were crowded by passengers and luggage, coils of rope lay about and set landsmen wondering at their uses, trusses of hay, squeezed by machinery into such a state of solidity that it looked almost possible to put a fine polish upon them, were strewed about in the most complete disorder. Two cows were bellowing in their cribs, cocks were crowing, geese were cackling, and pigs squeaking, children crying, emigrants shouting, and sailors singing at their work. Such was the state of the vessel when Captain Blomeskull came on board with the pilot, and the order was given to "weigh anchor."

Those who had remained on board to see the last of their relations and friends, took a sorrowful leave and returned to the shore. By the time the sails were set, the ship contained only those, excepting the pilot and his boat's crew, who were to brave in her, for four long months, the perils of the "great deep." The wind was favourable, and the shades of night soon hid the already indistinct shores of Britain from sight. Many an eye which closed in sleep that night, was shut for ever upon the fairest and happiest land in God's wide world.

CHAPTER II.

WE shall leave the passengers of the "Big Ann" to get over their sea sickness as best they can, whilst we return for a time to Mr. Raymond's cottage.

A few weeks have passed since Hugh's departure—it was evening—the little parlour was occupied by the father and his two daughters. Many conjectures and guesses were being made as to the exact latitude the "Big Ann" had reached. Mr. Raymond was appealed to, and unrolling a well-thumbed chart, pointed out the very spot where he had no doubt she might at that moment be found—rather a bold assertion for an old navigator to make; but it had the effect intended, for the sisters pictured, in their simplicity, the delight Hugh would experience on the morrow when he sighted the Canary Islands.

"Do you know," said Annie Raymond, after a short pause in the conversation, "Hugh has been away only a few weeks, and Amy Leslie has asked me, very often, if we have heard from him. I think she loves him nearly as well as we do."

"Before Hugh left us," said Kate, "she said his pride made him leave England, and that she feared because he was poor he fancied himself not so worthy of her regard; but that for her part, she should never marry for the sake of money. I told Hugh, and he said his mind was made up to go abroad; but that had he known exactly the state of Amy's affections earlier, it might have delayed his coming to such a decided resolution.—'It would have been a great temptation for me to have remained in England,' he said, 'for Amy is wealthy: she is a good, affectionate girl, and I was always fond of her; and I must confess, now that I am going to leave you all, that I feel more love for her than friendship. But then I am poor and proud. I will become more her equal in wealth than I am at present; and I will not sell my independence even when inclination most strongly tempts me.'"

Hugh fancied himself a philosopher: he had no idea that a love of adventure, and the gratification of a naturally roving disposition, went hand in hand with a spirit of independence, and urged him to take the step he did. Thrown together as Miss Leslie and he had been from early life, it is hardly surprising that an attachment existed between them. It had grown so imperceptibly, that Hugh had never directly spoken of love until they were on the point of parting; then he told her he should return to England in four years, and hoped to find her the same dear girl he was leaving. Promises to correspond passed on both sides, and so the lovers parted.

There is a great sameness in all long voyages, and it is not our intention to bore the reader with a nautical log, but merely to record the most interesting events which befell the "Big Ann" and some of her passengers.—She was three weeks out of Plymouth—the Bay of Biscay passed—sea sickness had disappeared, and every thing on board went on in a regular routine. She had experienced fine weather and fair breezes. Hugh found his companions, with a few exceptions, agreeable and well-bred men. A case of sickness was reported in the steerage, and the "doctor" (every man of physic soon attains his degree on board ship) pronounced it typhus. The sick man grew worse and worse. He was brought on deck, where an awning was spread over him, and every attention possible was paid to the poor sufferer, but he died in a few days in the arms of his wife and daughter, leaving them without a protector.

The friends of the deceased, who was an Irish Catholic, would not allow the Protestant Chaplain on board to read prayers over the body. The day he died he was buried. The sun shone down brightly and the water was calm, clear, and deeply blue. Not a word was uttered as the corpse was brought to the gangway sewn in canvass and laid on a grating, with the union jack for a pall. A common sympathy for death seemed to unite all, both Catholics and Protestants, then. The crew and passengers stood uncovered at the ship's side. A gesture was the only signal given, and the corpse slid from the grating and faded into "the remarkable silence of the grave," amid the unuttered prayers and ill-suppressed sobs of the mourners.

Having sighted the Cape de Verde and several other Islands, all went on prosperously until they neared the Cape of Good Hope. The wind had increased greatly during the day, and sail after sail had been taken in, and others reefed, until only a very little canvass remained set. The sea was rising, and there was every indication of the continuance of foul weather. Now arose the first gale of wind experienced since leaving port. The sailors talked of the " Flying Dutchman," as they cowered under any thing which afforded the least shelter. The carpenter was ordered to batten down the hatches, as the water was streaming down below from every wave that broke over the deck, which now frequently happened. The sky was obscured by heavy clouds which flew before the gale. Large masses of vapour rose to windward and broke into various and fantastic forms, presenting rich food to a fanciful imagination. A sea swept the cook's caboose and a portion of the bulwarks away together, and the probabilities of any cooked food for some days seemed very slight. The vessel was running before the wind and sea: it was now too late to permit her being hove to, and she sped wildly forward upon her course: three seamen were at the wheel, and it required their united efforts to prevent the " Big Ann " from broaching to. She rolled tremendously, her timbers creaked, and her whole frame trembled beneath the combined influence of the elements. A shriek of fear from those below was occasionally heard above the din of the storm: there were few of them who did not think that they were *in extremis,* and every shock the vessel sustained was the signal for a fresh outcry. The gale continued with unabated fury, and Hugh and his companions lay down in their clothes anxiously waiting for the morning. About three o'clock the vessel gave some tremendous lurches, and every article in the cabin seemed imbued with instant life—chests, boxes, tins, mess-water kegs, and some few articles of crockery were smashed against each other—" up the middle and back again;" and in the midst of the uproar, the fastenings of the port which was over Hugh's berth gave way, and a torrent of water dashed into the cabin. Hugh endeavoured to close the opening but it was useless, and in a short time the floor and those who occupied it were com-

pletely flooded. The higher tier of sleepers were more fortunate, and from Slinger's bunk something like a snore might
have been heard but for the din of the storm. The carpenter
succeeded in closing the port effectually without disturbing
Slinger.—" Well," he said, looking at him, "perhaps that man
aint a whole team of himself at a nap."

Hugh followed the carpenter and contrived to reach the
hatchway after scrambling over all sorts of impediments, for
every thing seemed to have changed places. He had scarcely
got his head above the level of the deck, when there was a cry
that the rudder band had got foul or broken, and that the vessel would not steer. The grandeur of the scene at this moment made him nearly overlook the perils which surrounded
him. The sky was clearer, and as he steadied himself, he could
see the long seas rolling after the ship in endless succession ;
their crested tops blown into spray by the fury of the wind,
which literally screeched through the rigging. The mainsail
split with a great noise, and in a few moments was lashed into
shreds. The captain was on deck, his white hair streaming in
the wind, but he stood calm and collected, giving directions to
secure the rudder again : the vessel then broached to. She
rode easier for a moment, and then settled in a trough of the
sea. A tremendous wave struck her as Hugh was descending
the hatchway, and he heard the captain shout " Hold on, my
lads—for your lives." Then followed a shock as if every timber of the vessel was being wrenched asunder, and a flood of
water swept Hugh off his legs, and left him on the floor of the
intermediate saloon, where he rolled about almost as helpless as
the numerous articles which the storm had torn from their fastenings : he succeeded in getting again on his legs, and scrambling to the deck, reached the captain's side, who roared his
commands through a trumpet, as the ship lay over appa-

D

rently unlikely to right again. "Now is the time—lay hold
on that rope," said the skipper to Hugh, and with "a long
pull, and a strong pull," the rudder band was cleared.—The
captain seized the wheel, and in a few moments the "Big
Ann" rode over the seas in comparative ease. The water below was rushing from side to side as if seeking for an exit—the
lower (and wet) berths had been tenantless for some time, their
late occupiers having relinquished them in favor of the dry dining table. The mate now informed the passengers that every
thing was right again, and the gale not increasing.

"I say, Mr. Moriarty," said Slinger, "this bunk of mine
aint the most uncomfortable six feet by two and a half in the
ship. Suppose you make my compliments to the poor old captain, who has been washed out from below, and tell him (as he
is rather spare) that if he will promise to lay only on his side
I'll let him stow with me." The mate executed Slinger's request, and presently the captain squeezed himself into Slinger's
berth. "Close stowage, captain," he said, "but never mind—
are you fond of music?" and Slinger, without waiting for an
answer, pulled a small flute from under his mattress, sat himself upon the edge of his bunk, and played several lively airs.—
"Pretty, aint it, cap'n." "Beautiful," replied he, as he wiped
his lips after withdrawing them from the mouth of a black bottle.—"Are you fond of grog, Slinger?" "Certainly, in moderation," was the answer.

"Well, then, take a moderate swig out of my bottle.—
When I was in the Peninsula"—

"No," interrupted Slinger, "no: thank you: I can't stand
a yarn now; but I'll drink your health with all my heart."

Having gone through this interesting ceremony, the cork
was secured, and the captain again placed the bottle safely underneath his head and soon fell asleep.

Hugh now came below and was hailed by Slinger, who set to work rumaging his wearing apparel from under the mattress, and so disturbed the old captain, who, however, only admonished him to "take care of the bottle," and fell a snoring again. "There!" said Slinger," as he reached the floor, "you jump into my warm place: you must have been up nearly all night." Hugh did not hesitate, but insinuated himself by degrees into Slinger's old quarters.

"I was woke up," said Slinger, "by the rolling of the ship, and those noisy rascals in the steerage kept me awake for a bit.—Only listen! do you hear that fellow singing 'My ship is my boast and my home's the wild main?' he was at prayers not very long ago, but now that he has swallowed all his week's allowance of grog, he's grown quite valiant :—by Jove I'll leave you to sleep, and I'll see if there is not some fun to be got out of him." Saying which, the flute was again put into requisition, and Hugh fell asleep with a vague idea that somebody was dancing something like a sailor's hornpipe in the next cabin.

The gale "blew itself out," to use a nautical expression, in three days, and was succeeded by several weeks of fine weather, during which time the chief amusements of the passengers were catching albatrosses with a hook baited with pork, and shooting the pretty little Cape pigeons which abound in most parts of the southern ocean. Thousands of miles from land these little rovers are observed following the ship for days together, with their gigantic companions the albatrosses, picking up any scraps of meat which happen to be cast overboard. Several whales were also seen in these latitudes.

At length the "Big Ann" entered Bass' Straits—four months after leaving England, and many were the congratulations which passed at the anticipated speedy termination of the voyage; for another week would probably see them in Port Philip, but that evening a contrary wind blew, and that very strongly. The vessel was hove to for the night, and the passengers were again in tribulation: not without reason; for, at the time we write, the navigation of Bass' Straits was but imperfectly known.

Wilson's promontory is a large tract of land on the south coast of New Holland, and the most southerly point of that large island; it runs upwards of sixty miles into the sea. The "Big Ann" had drifted far inside the point. In the morning the man at the look out reported high land ahead of the vessel. The wind was blowing directly ashore, and had she kept on the course she was then steering for half an hour longer, she must have been a wreck. She was put about, and every exertion used to beat her off the coast; but, in consequence of shoal water and sand banks, short tacks were obliged to be made, and by the afternoon the most inexperienced eye could perceive that nothing had been gained by the manœuvres. A consultation was held by the officers, and it was decided that nothing could be done but to spread all the sail she could carry, and so endeavour to clear the point. She was very light— much too light to sail well, and as a natural consequence made considerably more lee way than usual. Mean time the steerage passengers had come on deck in great numbers, and, impeding the work, they were ordered below. The hatches were battened down for the second time during the voyage. The ship struggled through the waters, leaving a long line of foam to mark her track.

"Does her head lay well outside the point?" cried the captain. "No:" answered the steersman, only just clears it." "Set more sail," shouted the captain: although the masts were bending and straining as if every freshening breeze would

have sent them over the side. More sail was set however, and
the "Big Ann" lay well outside the point. "If the sticks
and the ropes will only do their work for a quarter of an hour
longer," whispered Mr. Moriarty to Hugh, "we shall be right."
Almost before he had finished speaking, the main-top gallant
mast went with a crash, and the vessel fell off a few points.
"Are the anchors all ready Mr. Moriarty?" cried the captain,
"All clear, Sir," was the answer. "Very good," said the captain, as he took his stand by the wheel: "we have done all we
can, Providence must do the rest.—How's her head?" "Well
outside the point, now Sir, but she drops off every now and
again." Two men were stationed at the hatches with orders to
tear them up the moment there was any imminent danger. One
of the men sat himself down, put a bit of rope in his mouth
and chewed it with all apparent signs of coolness. The passengers were making a great noise below, and he growled out,
"Lie quiet, can't ye? isn't it as well to go down quietly as
kicking up sich a bobbery?—I'm blest if this aint the last voyage I'll make in an emigrant ship—a slaver's nothing to it."
Certainly it did not appear by any means impossible that the
present voyage would close Jack's nautical career; for the vessel was within a quarter of a mile of the shore, and she appeared to be nearly surrounded by sand banks; the noise of
the waves beating on the rock-bound coast was painfully dis-
tinct, and the long unbroken line of foam showed but too
clearly the fate which awaited the ship unless the point could
be cleared.

"I think," said the captain, after a pause, to the mate,
who was steering, "that she's all right this time; ten minutes
will decide it." "It's close shaving," said the mate. All on
deck felt the peril they were in: none knew it better than the
captain and the mate; but they were collected, and gave the

few orders requisite with full confidence of their being obeyed, for they were both favourites with the seamen.

Mean time the men stationed at the hatches conversed in whispers, their eyes anxiously directed to the shore. "It's a bad job, I'm afeard," said the latter of the two; "if we strike what'll become of the passengers?—our boats wont hold a quarter on'em." "Strike! be blowed," said the other; "d'ye see, we are almost abreast of the point?" "And do you see," said his companion, "that we could almost chuck a biscuit ashore?"

It was not many minutes before the mate resigned the wheel into the hands of the man from whom he had taken it, he and the captain shook hands heartily, and well they might, for the point was cleared, and the danger left behind; sail was reduced, and then the men were ordered a double allowance of grog.

A fresh hand now came aft to the wheel—"A close shave just now, Bill: eh?', he said.

"Aye: 'twas uncommon—thought of Davy Jones:—a miss is as good as a mile, though; and 'tis an ill wind that blows nobody good:—it's blowed us a double allowance of grog—there's consolation in that. I ony wish 't'ad blowed us some baccy; for I don't think there's a pound in all the ship, cept wot the long passenger's got, and that's pretty nigh spoilt, for its cigars."

"Oh here he comes on deck! just fetch me a wad of hay, will you? and I'll try and torture some compassion out of him."

The passenger referred to now came on the poop. He was a tall high-shouldered man, who stooped a great deal, and wore spectacles.

The steersman having been supplied with a wisp of hay, rolled it up tightly, and pushing one end into his cheek he chewed away upon it as if it were his natural food. The passenger walked up and down several times, then lit a cigar, and continued his exercise. It was not until Jack had been seized with several very violent fits of coughing that the object of his exertions bestowed the least attention on him; he then advanced, and noticing some strange and unusual substance protruding from the man's mouth, he wiped his spectacles, and regarding him with amazement for a time, exclaimed, " Why what on earth are you eating my good fellow ? "

" Nuffin thir : I'm chawing."

" Chewing what ? " said the astonished passenger.—" It *is* hay ! ", he said in a positive tone, after a minute examination.

" Yes," said Jack in a melancholy voice, "it is hay, and no mistake—worse luck ; " and then he whispered in a very confidential tone, as if the sad fact were a secret to all else on board, " there a'int an ounce of baccy in the ship, Sir."

" Indeed ! " said the passenger : " No tobacco, Eh ? Could you make shift with a cigar, do you think ? "

" Try me," replied Jack, with a knowing wink at his comrade, who was enjoying the success of the trick.

Just at this juncture one of the petty officers came on deck— he was no favourite—and addressing the tall passenger said, " No talking to the man at the wheel, if you please, Sir ." and turning round sharply to the steersman, he exclaimed, " D—e what kind of steering d'ye call this ?—where are you taking the vessel to ?—what's her course ? "

" I'm hard o'hearing," replied Jack.

" I said, where are you taking the ship to ? " bawled out the petty officer : " and what course are you steering ? "

" Taking her ! " said Jack with well assumed surprise, " I'm a taking of her from the port o'London to the port o'Melbourne, and her course is sow west by sow, Sir," said Jack : whose temper was ruffled by the loss of the tobacco which appeared all but in his grasp, or rather between his teeth. The petty officer left the poop, and the tall passenger gave the steersman a couple of cigars.

"Thank you, Sir, kindly," he said, "you'll scarcely believe that I've been redooced to the needcessity of chawing old junk, with straw and hay for wariety's sake, until (here he became quite confidential again) I actilly felt summat going wrong in my breadbasket.—Ah! Sir, it's a fact I'm telling on you," and a melancholy shake of the head confirmed it.

The tall passenger appeared moved at the recital of Jack's utter destitution—"poor fellow!" he said, as he turned away to continue his exercise.

"Before you go," said Jack, "may I be so bould as to ax you, respectfully, o'course, Sir, and not meaning no harm, just to sniggle up the ends o'your cigars in this here little article (handing a steel tobacco box) when you've done with 'em and can't smoke 'em no shorter: perhaps they may hact as a hantidote to the junk."

"No! no!" said the good natured passenger in evident disgust:—"no, I say," as Jack thrust the box into his hand: "I'll give you a cigar now and then instead."

"May you never want baccy, Sir, nor a glas o'grog to wash your mouth with when you've been using it," said Jack, taking a portion of one of the cigars from his mouth and carefully depositing the same in his box. The tall passenger, however, did not take the hint intended, as conveyed in Jack's words and actions.

CHAPTER III.

OUR preface pledges us to a true account of an emigrant's course: the varying details which we have inflicted on the reader, must be excused in this conscientious fulfilment of our profession. The foregoing is indeed nothing but what every emigrant must make up his mind to endure (unless he goes out as a cabin passenger,) e'er he reach El Dorado and fortune. Some high flown descriptions make the voyage appear more like a pleasure trip in my lord's yacht; but seriously, reader, salt junk will be thy chief animal food, biscuits must serve thee in lieu of bread, and Boreas won't always (even to oblige cabin passengers,) restrain his might.

The long wished-for land was at last in sight, and though it appeared but a long low line of coast, broken here and there by a pyramidal shaped hill, each eye, bent upon it, was finding beauties, which to a landsman's sight would have been very questionable indeed. The ship neared the shore, and sailed along the coast for a time, until a narrow opening was detected with a ledge of rocks running some distance across it: this was the entrance to Port Philip. On the opposite side the high land of Arthur's Seat could be distinctly seen in the distance; whilst the adjacent coast consisted of low shelving rocks, with barren sand-hillocks behind. A bold headland marked where the deepest water was to be found. There were several vessels in sight steering for the Port Philip heads, and others dropping out with the tide, even against the wind, which was blowing fresh from the southward, and fair for entering.

The "Big Ann" was about a mile off the mouth of the

C

port when the tide began to tell against her, but as the breeze freshened considerably, it was considered advisable to attempt the passage without delay. The ship was soon in the ripple occasioned by the wind and tide being in contrary directions. She laboured and struggled to get on, seemingly held back by some invisible power, like a steed eager to dash forward, but restrained by the strong arm of its rider. Her sails remained full, excepting when some huge uprising mass of water lifted her, and for the moment rendered her rudder useless; still she held her own, and plunged into the big waves—not over them: it looked almost like a personal contest between two combatants nearly matched. The wind continued to freshen, and the vessel gained ground: it lulled for a moment or two, and the boiling sea bore her back upon its bosom. Whirlpools appeared, and were as quickly gone, for a great wave rolling in from the ocean, would leave the water momentarily smooth. Presently some strange commotion appeared to be taking place beneath, a great bubbling mass of water would rise, apparently capable of overwhelming the largest ship, and subside as mysteriously as it had arisen. Such is the passage into Port Philip, in certain states of the wind and tide.

After ineffectually attempting the passage for several hours, the tide having spent its chief force, the ship slowly accomplished the long anticipated end, and the expanse of water which met the view inside the heads, sufficiently accounted for the extraordinary resistance to the ship's progress; for as far as the eye could reach up the bay (it almost deserves the name of a sea), was a sheet of water, dotted here and there by sand banks, and mud islands; and the only exit for it all was the one, two miles broad, through which we have just navigated the "Big Ann."

Patches of the shores of Port Philip were visible at some distance to the N. E., whilst on the point forming the eastern entrance, a few huts could be discovered along the shore, and some hills in the back ground covered with luxuriant verdure and crowned with trees. The sea-sick eyes of the passengers dwelt upon the landscape with that delight which possibly only a painter may partially comprehend : four months upon the ocean however, will discover many beauties in nature, which else must remain hidden. Dark sombre woods, which clothed parts of the coast, even to the water's edge, were pronounced "beautiful" and "enchanting;" but forty miles of the same view became monotonous; and by the time they had neared Hobson's Bay, the effect was no more than if so much green baize had been spread before the weary eyes that were tracing the vessel's progress.

The setting sun witnessed the "Big Ann" laying tranquilly at anchor off Williamstown—the port of Melbourne. Thank God, the last of the 16,000 miles was completed. The regular Government officers came on board, and the ship being pronounced healthy, the emigrants were told to prepare themselves for engagements on the morrow. There was great carousing that night in all parts of the ship. Early the next morning her decks were crowded with persons anxious to engage servants.

The captain was gone ashore with his papers, and the stout and pompous colonial magistrate, whose company we have avoided during the voyage, was strutting about the poop in all his overgrown dignity. The mate and he had only exchanged a few words since the commencement of the voyage, and those not of the most courteous or friendly nature. Mr. Moriarty seeing him alone, said to him, "Mr. Robberson, the time is

come at last for you to put your threat into execution, I mean
regarding the six dozen you once dared to say you would give
me if you had me in the colonies—there, Sir, is a rope, begin ·"
and the mate, thrusting a rope into Mr. Robberson's hand, presented his broad back in an attractive attitude for flagellation.
"Come, Sir," said the mate to his unwilling antagonist, who
was so overcome with conflicting feelings (in which fear and
cowardice held the predominance), that he remained speechless,
and although with the rope in his hand, he looked very much
more like a man who was going to receive a castigation, than
to give one.   "Perhaps, Sir," continued the mate, "it may be
more agreeable to your feelings to give me a written apology."
The great-little man began stammering out something intended
to mollify the mate's wrath, but it had the contrary effect; for
he proceeded coolly to tuck up his sleeves :—this demonstra-
tion induced Mr. Robberson to say, "I—really I have no intention—I don't wish to give anybody a thrashing."

"And do you fancy, Mr Robberson, that I'll take *that* for
an apology?"

"What more can you expect from a Colonial Magistrate?"
said he.

The mate smote upon a hen's coop with his heavy fist and
split in the top—"I expect nothing from such magistrates as
you but what would disgrace any Bench but a Colonial one, in
proof of which assertion," continued he, "I shall expect you
to sign this," and he produced from his pocket a slip of paper, and fetched a pen from the cabin

Mr. Robberson was dodging below, but was met part way by
the mate. The stout man looked far more like a convict than
one who had been accustomed to sit in judgment on that unfortunate class.

"Now," said the mate, spreading the writing materials upon the hen-coop, "do you mean to sign that paper or"— and he cast his eye towards the rope.

"Well," stammered out Mr. Robberson, "if I must, I must;" and he set himself to write with the same elaborate attention to attitude as Mr. Samuel Weller, Junior, displayed when he edited his ever memorable "Wallentine to Mary Housemaid at Mr. Nupkins Mayor."

Mr. Moriarty received the paper folded from Mr. Robberson, and as he placed it in his pocket, said, "You colonial aristocrats derive great benefit from your voyages to civilized countries: you have been taught a lesson which you will never forget.—Good day, Sir," and he turned upon his heel.

Mr. Robberson hailed the first passing boat, in which, with his wife, he left the ship. After he had got well out of harm's way, he shouted to Mr. Moriarty, who was leaning over the bulwark, and placing himself in the same attitude in which the savages are described by Defoe as saluting Robinson Crusoe, he roared, at the top of his voice, "Let me catch you ashore, you tyrant—you fellow—you—you—you—"

"Pooh!—pooh!—pooh:" said the mate, as he held the written apology aloft.

"Yes! I see, you scoundrel;" said the magistrate, just see what you have got, although you *did* put me in fear for my life, but I'll trounce you for it.—See what it's worth, you hound;"—and a sneering laugh followed.

The mate withdrew into his cabin, and opening the paper he had drawn up, found, instead of the magistrate's signature thereto, certain characters, which, after some difficulty, he deciphered, and burst into a loud laugh—"The rascal has done me," he said, as he scribbled at the foot of the paper this note "Specimen of writing by a colonial aristocrat:"—"but I'll have it framed and glazed, and hung up in my cabin." It was framed, and probably hangs there to this day: would that it was displayed in a more conspicuous place, and could have the effect of humbling the false "dignity of an illiterate, narrow minded, purse proud, heartless colonial aristocracy—one of the most intolerable nuisances on the face of the earth."*

In a very short time all the emigrants who were so disposed, had engaged themselves at what would appear in England ridiculously high wages. Bricklayers, masons, and mechanics of all descriptions, made their own terms; for the demand far exceeded the supply. One fortunate settler, who had come down from that extensive place "somewhere in the interior," had succeeded in engaging twelve men as shepherds, and he was reviewing his little band with signs of satisfaction; and because he was a good specimen of the men who make Australia respectable, we will give a full length portrait of him. He was of moderate height, muscular, and active. Those portions of his face which were not hidden by his moustaches and beard, might be pronounced handsome; his eyes were quick and penetrating, and his whole bearing was that of a gentleman in a strange but not unbecoming dress. He was quite at home amongst the motley crew who surrounded him —courteous and communicative to all: no doubt he would have been equally at his ease in a drawing room. His brows were shaded by a broad-brimmed manilla hat. His throat was partially covered by the extremities of his huge beard, which clouds of tobacco smoke could not entirely hide: what was seen of

---

* Dr. Lang

It must not be considered that there are many Mr Robbersons on the Australian Bench in these days He is only introduced as a type of a class of vain, ignorant, and vulgar upstarts, who have been thrown upon the surface of colonial society by accidental circumstances, and have managed to retain a place there, though in England they would not be tolerated for an hour

it was of a reddish colour from long exposure to a burning sun. His upper dress was a blouse made of a light material, fastened round the middle by a broad leather belt, on which depended a kangaroo-skin pouch, serving as a pocket for his pipe, tobacco, and tinder-box. His nether-man was clothed with a loose pair of canvass trousers, and he had low boots on his feet, which were devoid of socks or stockings.

But there was one obstinate fellow who would make no engagement on any terms (and he had many offers,) "on account," as he told Hugh, "of a little matter he was afther settling."

"And what may that be?" asked Hugh.

"It's a grate saycret, Misther Raymond, but I'm ingaged already, bother! but I'm in love; and there you have the whole of it."

"It's come to that, Mick, is it?" said Hugh.

"Yes: and how could I in conscience ingage myself twice over? and jist going to be married too, if there's a praist in the settlement."

"Has the lady any money?" enquired Hugh.

"Divel a scriddick, Mr. Hugh. Is it the money, d'ye think, I'de be afther marrying Rose Blaney for?"

"Oh no:" said Hugh, smiling: "Rose is a fortune in herself: but you forget, Mick:—what will you do as a married man?—You can't leave your wife and go into the bush."

"Lave *her!*—is it?" said Mick: "niver!"

"Then you know," continued Hugh, "marrying is expensive. First, there are fees to be paid; then you must have a house to take your wife to; then there must be something to keep the pot boiling; then in a few years you must expect little additions."—

"Whist! whist!" broke in Mick, "that'll do: sure what

a perspiration I'm in :—we never think of matters of that kind in Ireland, at all—at all, when we get married." Mick was plunged in deep thought for a short time, when he said, with his face as blank as his pocket, "Och! the divil a shilling have I: —och, what'll we do—och, what'll we do?" He rushed over to the hatchway, and calling "Here darlint come up and spake wid me," resumed his old position near Hugh. A woman shortly appeared from below, and running over to Mick, cried out, "Here I am, darlint;" and throwing both her arms round him, imprinted several fervent kisses on his astonished countenance.—"Sure thin, Mick—darlint, didn't I always think you loved me best?" Mick looked the picture of confusion. After being subjected to a second volley of kisses, he tore her arms from about him, and exclaimed, "Why what the dickens is the matther wid the woman?—go to yer rale sweetheart, and not be stormin 'me that way, and forgetting yearself this way, Mary O'Rourke."

"Och! wirra! wirra!" she said, turning to Hugh: "Sure that dirty blackguard, Tim Flannagan, has hired and gone into the bush amongst the schnakes and the neaygers, and left me upon the wide world, and now what'll I do that Mick has desarted me?" and she burst out crying.

Hugh really began to fancy that Mick had been playing the part of a "gay Lothario," and must have expressed as much in his countenance; for Mick exclaimed, "I was always noted for my gallanthry, Mr. Hugh; but by the hole in my coat (he might have sworn by the fifty holes in that garment) I never wronged the young woman:—Faith how could I, don't I love Rose Blaney dearly?—Why Mary O'Rourke," he continued, turning to that disconsolate creature, "don't be crying that way. sure if yer sweetheart's left you, like a blackguard as he is, you'll soon find another in his room."

"To be sure she will," said a rough-looking personage, who was lolling against the bulwarks smoking a black pipe, and if the young woman's agreeable, I think I know a gentleman who is on the look out for a wife; only he can't afford to waste much time in courting; he's not a bad looking fellow either—in fact," he said, with a knowing wink, "he's as like myself as two peas."

Mary O'Rourke wiped her tears at this information, and the "matrimonial advocate" pleaded so well, that before many days were over, Mary O'Rourke was known by another name.

Rose Blaney now came on deck, but was going below again, on seeing Mick and Hugh in earnest conversation: but Hugh beckoned her to come to them.

"Rose," said Hugh, "so you are going to be married?"

"Yes, Sir," she replied, with a courtesy, blushing and smiling kindly on Hugh.

"Now don't you think, Mick," said Hugh, "if you were to get a situation for Rose somewhere in Melbourne and go into service yourself for a few months, that you would be better prepared for matrimony?"

"Well, Sir," said Mick, "but you always was the kind gentleman, and I do suppose, as we haven't anything to get married on, that must be the way of it; but niver mind Rose, darlin," he said, embracing her, "sure I'll see you often and often."

"And now," said Hugh, "before we part, I have a little account to settle with you both for the work you have done for me on the way out: will a couple of pounds satisfy you?"

"A couple of what, Sir?" exclaimed Mick.

"Two pounds—forty shillings," replied Hugh.

"No," said Mick, disdainfully, "it won't."

"I'm sure I thought I had made you a fair offer," said Hugh

F

in a disappointed tone—for he attributed Mick's refusal to avarice.

"What we've done for you, Mr. Raymond, was done for love," said Mick · "you helped us when we could not help ourselves; and we have done as much for you.—A purty figure you'd have cut cleaning yer boots and washing yer shirts:" and he and Rose burst into a fit of laughing at the bare idea of his patron being engaged in such occupations.

Hugh was much pleased to find he had erred in his estimate of Mick's motives, and urgently pressed the money upon his acceptance; but he still refused. He was more successful with Rose, who took the proffered gold with a courtesy, spite of all Mick's winks and hints to her not to do so.

"Whist," she said, "havn't we lots of money now to get married, and can't we return the guineas to Misther Hugh when we've airned some?"

"Augh! lave the wimen alone for invinshun," said Mick, looking at his "darlin" in perfect admiration at this proof of her forethought and discretion. "I should niver have thought of that.—If you plaze, Sir," he continued, addressing Hugh, "Rose is much beholden to you, and—and—we mane to get married."

The mischief was past all remedy now; and the very next boat which left the ship, bore the loving couple ashore, who showered innumerable blessings on the head of their benefactor.

CHAPTER IV.

On going below to pack up his "goods and chattels," Hugh found Slinger similarly employed. They had become very intimate during the voyage; and now the time for parting appeared drawing near, Hugh felt deeply the loss he should sustain in his messmate, who was about his own age, an intelligent, merry-hearted companion, and who only required his friendship to be put to the test to prove its disinterestedness and sincerity. As Hugh entered the cabin, Slinger said to him, in a dolorous voice,

"I'm going ashore."

"So am I," said Hugh :—"we'll go together after stowing away our traps."

"Confound the things," said Slinger; adding several rough articles of clothing to an already well-filled chest, and pressing down the cover with all his might :—"I wish I understood packing."

"Jump it in," said Hugh, "I'll help you:" and the two friends getting upon the top of the chest, performed some eccentric movements which, however, had the effect desired; for Slinger was soon enabled to close and lock it easily.

"By the bye," he said, "I quite forgot—but I have several hats in that same chest."

"Capital stuff for gun wads," said Hugh : and after a pause, "Do you know, Slinger, my dear fellow, I shall be very sorry to part from you—very sorry."

"Strange coincidence," said Slinger, "but it's the very thing I have been thinking of all day.—*Must* we part?—why must we? I've a little money—not much to be sure; and an idea has frequently struck me of late, that we might do something together :—it seems to me as if we were cut out for partners—eh ? ”

“ My capital is anything but large,” said Hugh, “ £150 is rather a small amount to commence any business with, excepting that of match or broom merchant.”

“ I've £200,” said Slinger, “ there's a clear £350 to start with.”

“ But mine is a much less sum than your's, Slinger; so if we do anything together, you must put £50 into a bank, if there is one in Melbourne, in your own name.”

“ Oh !—oh !—yes of course I must,” said Slinger, at the same time with a “ mental reservation ” to do nothing of the sort. Would that all “ mental reservations ” could boast of such disinterested and pure motives.

“ Hugh Raymond and Co., General Merchants,” he continued.—“ Is it a bargain ?—*Yes*. then give me your hand my boy.” The spirit of honesty seemed to bind those hands together as if loath to part them, for they continued their grasp for some minutes. Then Slinger proceeded, addressing himself to the now deserted berths, “ If any of you know any just cause or impediment why these two persons should' not be joined together in the bonds of partnership, why out with it.—No answer ? Well, that's settled : ” and picking up a piece of chalk, which was lying on the floor of the cabin, he wrote several times, as he said, just to get his hand in, “ Raymond & Co.”

“ No ! no ! ” said Hugh, “ it shall be Slinger and Co.”

The point admitted of argument:—so it was left to chance.—

“ Head or tail,” said Slinger, producing a shilling.—“ Tail —you lose, henceforth I shall be known as the Co.; and there's an end of that.—Signed, sealed, and delivered on board the ‘ Big Ann,’ this nineteenth day of July—and all that

kind of thing;" and the two friends and partners again shook
hands warmly; nor did the informality of their contract affect
its being adhered to with integrity.

"What a splendid climate!" exclaimed Slinger, putting his
head out of the port to enjoy the refreshing breeze, and then
"By all that's powerful but there's something very like a steamer coming up astern."

Their preparations being all completed, they went on deck.
A steamer was nearing them and a very small one too—a very
Tom Thumb of steamers. After wheezing and puffing a great
deal, the movement of the machinery being aided by the captain,
who acted also as engineer, and added his own exertions to the
two-and-a-half horse power of the engine, she was brought
alongside to receive passengers. She was called the "Leviathan;" and was not the only example the Colony afforded of
very contemptible things bearing magniloquent names.

The "Leviathan" having received three passengers, consisting of Hugh, Slinger, and a Mr. Weevel (a cabin passenger), and their luggage, started for the mouth of the Yarra—
the town of Melbourne being situated on the left bank of that
river, and by water, some five or six miles from the bay.

Mr. Weevel was a gentleman who had left England without
any definite notion of the description of country to which he
was consigning himself. He had once read a glowing work on
India (Mr. W. was not a great reader), and his mind had
never since been entirely free from the impression that all British possessions were necessarily somewhat alike. The idea he
had conceived of Australia was that of a country where luxuri-
ous natives sat under shady groves by day, sipping oriental
drinks and smoking *genuine* cigars; this pleasant life varied
occasionally by a tiger hunt, in which the sportsman was effectually removed from all danger by being stationed in a strongly

fortified castle borne on the back of a gigantic elephant. In short, Australia to him was to have been a sensual paradise. But he had, even already, seen and heard sufficient to excite in the little mind he possessed sensations of doubt, disappointment, and dismay. He was dressed in the most extravagant style, for he did not lack money; and like most men of small minds, was, even in the most inappropriate situations, parading the fact before the world.

The "Leviathan" had reached about half way to her destination, when the engine gave evident signs of being out of order. The captain, by uniting his strength with its failing powers, succeeded for a time in keeping the boat in motion. The inevitable climax came at last. Puff-puff—puff-puff—pu—ff—then a full stop; and the helpless "Leviathan" drifted to the bank of the river.

"Stir up the fire, Jim," cried the skipper.

"'Taint no good, commodore," said the boy, who acted as crew and stoker, and was on easy terms with his superior officer, "there's someat wrong with her biler."

"'Twont burst, will it?" exclaimed Mr. Weevel, retreating two steps—another, and he would have been overboard. "If it should burst—oh dear!—oh dear!—Mr. Slinger—Mr. Raymond—do you think we are in danger?"

"Raymond & Co., if you please, Mr. Weevel; that is the style of our firm. *We* do not think there is any present danger; indeed, *we* think if the boiler were to burst, we should be quite safe," said Slinger, grinning, and appealing to Hugh for confirmation of what he said, and laying particular stress upon the plural pronoun.

"Oh thank you I'm sure—thank you," said Weevel, "allow me to —" he was going to say "shake hands with you," but observing Slinger's hands were rather dirty (for he had lent his aid, hoping to keep the broken-down engine up to its work), Mr. Weevel simply added, "to—to congratulate you."

The captain went below, if going below it could be called, where half his body was exposed above the deck, and was heard muttering as to the utter impossibility of getting the engine to work in its present state. "And so," he said, stepping upon the deck, "as there's no wind, there's nothin for it but treeing her up."

"Goodness me!" said poor Weevel, who appeared to have made up his mind that some dreadful catastrophe was about to happen, and that "treeing her up" was only another term for "blowing her up."

The skipper explained that his process was of a far less expeditious nature; and proceeded to put it in execution. A rope was got out forward and fastened at its extreme length to a convenient tree, when the skipper, aided by his passengers, hauled away upon it until his craft was drawn up to the tree, then the rope was again taken on, and the same thing repeated.

"Slow work this," said Slinger to Weevel, as the "Leviathan" got entangled among some branches which had fallen into the Yarra, but poor Weevel's attention was engaged on another subject.

"I feel very curious," he said,—"very curious indeed:—I hope the vessel is clean: but my face itches in a most extraordinary manner ·—it must be the gnats," said Weevel,—"what numbers of them there are!" and he made repeated dabs at his persecutors as they pitched upon his face and forehead.

"Gnats," said the skipper—"them aint gnats; them's musqueeters, and you'll find 'em uncommon interestin little creeters, I tell you;—they are allers partial to new chums too."

But Mr. Weevel was not the only victim; for each passen-

ger suffered more or less. Every exposed portion of the body
became the ground of contest; and although hundreds of mosquitoes were crushed, it was a hopeless case to expect to end
the persecution, as thousands appeared in their room.

"I"ll tell you what, passengers," said the captain, "if you
scratch and bang yourselves about as you're doing, you'll spile
your beauty. As for you, young man," turning to Mr. Weevel,
"your mother would hardly know you as it is."

"Ah," whined Weevel, "she little thinks how confoun-
dedly her Augustus is taken in, and will soon be done
for.—Ah!" this exclamation was accompanied by a sound slap
on the cheek administered by himself, in a futile effort to an-
nihilate one of the pests: if some one else had slapped Mr.
Weevel's face he could scarcely have exclaimed more passion-
ately, "that I should ever have subjected myself to this!"

The "Leviathan" was again moving through the water
steadily, for a breeze had sprung up, and the only sail she could
boast was set to catch it as it sighed through the tall tea-tree
scrubs which lined the river's banks.

"Is all the country like this?" said Weevel, in a despond-
ing tone.

"Oh! no:—some's like that," replied the captain, as he
pointed to a swamp which could just be distinguished through
the scrub.—"D'ye like it better, lad?" said the skipper with
a grin.

Mr. Weevel regarded the prospect for a moment, and then
sunk his head in utter despair.

"He's a nice fellow to come to a new country," whispered
Slinger, "a few mosquitoes, a scrub, and a swamp have broken his spirit—that is, if he ever had one."

The mosquitoes became more blood-thirsty that ever. Poor
Weevel was endeavouring to wrap his face in a highly scented

and particularly white handkerchief. He had taken off his hat and placed it on the deck, when the sun, reflected from a small circular looking-glass, which was fixed inside the crown, cast the glitter full in the skipper's eyes.

"Bust my biler!" he exclaimed with an uncommonly near approach to an oath,—"why what on airth's that?" and starting forward, leaving the vessel to take her chance, looked into the hat in the most perfect wonderment. "Well," he said, " I'm blest if it aint a beautiful contrivance to skear the natives—Ha!—ha!—ha!"

Mr. Weevel appeared to have resigned himself to any fate which might await him. The skipper's hearty laugh somewhat roused him, and divesting himself of the handkerchief, he recovered his hat and regarded himself steadfastly in the glass. His face was covered with red blotches, his eyelids swollen, his forehead lacerated, his hair in disorder, and his shirt bloody: it was no wonder he gazed at himself in horror.

"I told you, you'd spoil your beauty," said the captain: " why didn't you listen to an old hand, like the other gentlemen, eh? It's no use your staring that way into the hat, as if you was trying to look a hole through the crown."

Mr. Weevel still looked on—after a short interval his hat fell from his hands, and, with a deep sigh, he laid himself out upon the deck.

Both Hugh and Slinger were somewhat concerned at the state poor Weevel was in, and kindly raised him from where he lay, and endeavoured to alleviate his distresses; but he was not to be comforted until the scrubs and the mosquitoes were left behind.

"Oh!" said Weevel, after some time, "I will return and write a true account of this abominable place, so different from what I once read."

G

As Weevel had partially recovered, Hugh could not resist the temptation of saying "Of course you will write from experience—make a work of three volumes—call it 'A Peep into the Interior of Australia Felix; comprising a Voyage up the Yarra, and a Natural History of the Mosquitoes.' You might make the world aware of your acute perception, by adding, that all your information was obtained during a *five hours'* excursion."

"Only be careful," interrupted Slinger, "that you don't spoil the chance of those who of necessity must remain here."

"Oh ! I'm demd !" said Weevel, as he caught the reflection of his disfigured face in his looking-glass—"Dem the moschitoes—dem the colony—dem every thing."

"What a dreadful hand you'd be for swearing, Sir," said the captain, "if you could only speak plain."

Mr. Weevel expressed anger in his looks, as far as his countenance was capable of showing it, but the swollen face assumed a grotesque smile when Slinger, directly appealing to Weevel's weakness, observed, that "there would be one extraordinary fact connected with Mr. Weevel's book—the author would be a rich one."

"The next turn of the river, gentlemen," said the skipper, "and you'll see Melbourne "

Then it was that the passengers became acutely sensible of their sluggish progress. On reaching that part of the Yarra indicated, several low huts were seen, on either bank of the river, standing close to the water's edge On a beautiful green hill (Bateman's Hill), which rose on their left they could distinguish a building of a better class ; further up the stream, and on a parallel line with it, were several edifices built of brick ; but the greater part of the best houses were of weather-

board.   There were also some very doubtful-looking erec-
tions, unlike dwellings, but too good for piggeries.   In reply
to an inquiry addressed to the captain, he informed his
passengers that they were merchants' stores.   Amongst the
buildings were large stumps, with the parent stems laid low
by their sides, cumbering the ground.   Gigantic trees dotted the undulating country in the distance, and with tents
pitched here and there made the back-ground of the picture.
Huge heaps of heavy timber, piled up high above some of the
humbler huts, were burning furiously, and dense columns of
smoke were so numerous, that one might easily have imagined
the town was on fire.   Thus does civilization mark her first in-
roads in a new country.

"Melbourne," said the captain in an introductory style,
pointing to the objects we have endeavoured to describe.

"Melbourne!" said Weevel,—"that Melbourne!! I have
a plan of the town here;"and he produced one from his pocket-
book.   "Pray point out the several churches marked on it.—
Where is the custom-house?—Where the gaol?—Where the
wharf?—Where is government-house?—the barracks?—the
police office?—and in short, where is the town?

"Easy," cried the skipper, "I'll point 'em all out to you
directly, ony give me time.—The shade of the largest trees
left standin are our churches for the present;" and he added
with more feeling than might have been looked for from him,
"and I tell you it's a pleasant thing, my lads, to hear the birds
a cherruppin away above, whilst we are praisin God below—
there's somethin very soothin in it arter one's been working
this here crazy craft up and down the stream to'ther six days
o'the week.   That little crib, a short way up from the Yarra, is
the custom-house.   We aint got no regler gaol because we haven't
wanted one yet—only a lock up, and I'll show you that by and

by," he said with a smile.—"Here's the wharf," he continued, as the steamer bumped against the river's bank. "Government house is not to be seen for trees; and up above there," he said, pointing to the top of a shingled roof which appeared above the water, "is the police office and lock-up, just under the falls d'ye see?"

"Under the falls!" said Hugh.

"Aye—that's the roof of it you see yonder with a hole in the top. Some of our jolly squatters—rough men, I tell you —being determined on a spree, thought the safest way to begin it would be to swamp the lock-up; and so being a pretty strong and united party, d'ye see, they defied the ten constables, stormed the police office, took it, and putting it on rolling logs of timber, they started it down the hill into the Yarra, and there 'tis now:—it nearly cost one or two of 'em their lives tho', for several of 'em would remain inside, and only saved themselves by tearing an opening in the roof.—Wild dogs!—wild dogs!" said the skipper, with a shake of his grey head;—"why that night they capsized half the wooden houses in the settlement."

"What a country to live in!" said Weevel: and this is the way the people in England are deceived?—Savages are called squatters;—sentry boxes, watch-houses and custom-houses; a mud bank, a wharf; pig-sties, dwelling houses;—trees, churches;—and —"

"Avast there, young man:" said the captain, getting warm at what he considered an unfair estimate of the infant colony: —"why you crawled afore you could walk, and had somebody to nuss you, I'll be bound; whilst we have had to take care of ourselves from the fust—with Sydney on one side always ready to shove the weakest to the wall, and to take any dirty advantage of us; and Adelaide upon t'other, with the English people bolsterin of it up, and sendin 'em out in ship loads, the bone and muscle we could better employ here.—Wait a bit—our turn's a comin—we'll square accounts with 'em both yet. When I came here fust, not many months agone, yonder hill was a pastur for kangaroo and a huntin-ground for the natives; now there's more business done there, rough as it looks, than in any place in England of ten times the size. The plan you are staring at, young man, is correct enough; only, it is what Melbourne is going to be—not exactly what it is. I'll just give it five years," said the captain, prophetically. At the termination of that period, Melbourne had attained that degree of importance which position and natural advantages had marked out for it.

CHAPTER V.

THE fare paid, our adventurers inquired of the captain what would be their best way of proceeding, and where they should deposit their luggage?

"Why," he said, "as to the matter of the luggage, get that put into some merchant's store; and, of course, at first you will stop at an inn—you haven't a tent. Suppose you try The Lamb.—Take care of your friend, there," he added to Hugh, as he pointed to Weevel:—poor fellow! he is uncommon green to be sure, and there's sharp customers in the settlement.—I'm a most afraid we shall have to put up a reglar quod here soon for some of 'em."

The luggage was piled on the bank, and Weevel directed to stand sentry over it, whilst Hugh and Slinger went in search of a conveyance of some kind, and to engage store-room. Weevel commenced his watchful duties by seating himself upon a box and mournfully examining his miserable self in the looking-glass in his hat; the result of the scrutiny seemed only to increase his wretchedness, and with a piteous sigh the unfortunate gentleman buried his face in his hands, and in that attitude remained.

Hugh's first object was, to find out the merchant upon whom his bill was drawn. He tried in vain to discover something like a street, but the houses and stores were spread about as if they had been each built as it best suited the whim of the proprietor. After some inquiry, they obtained from a colonist these rather peculiar directions:—"Carry the setting sun upon your left shoulders and the rising moon behind, and go straight on eend until you run your noses agin a post and rail fence—that's Binns's." Hugh looked in the man's face—there was no doubt he was seriously intending to direct the inquirers correctly and to the best of his abilities. Seeing they were new comers and rather puzzled to comprehend the instructions given, the goodnatured colonist set their faces in the direction he wished them to go, and went his way. After twenty minutes spent in tumbling over logs and such like impediments, our two friends were delighted to see before them a fence, and on a large board nailed against a tree " Binns, General Merchant." They soon discovered the store, and were fortunate in finding the owner within.

Having transacted their business, the merchant sent his horse and dray with them to bring up the boxes, previously exacting a promise that they would return with Weevel and dine. On reaching the wharf they found Weevel in nearly the same position in which they had left him—in fact he was asleep. A small party of natives had stationed themselves around him and

were regarding his singular appearance in silent wonderment.
The spectators were partially covered by opossum rugs, and
the portions of their bodies which were exposed were rudely
painted with a white substance, the effect of which upon the
black ground struck the new comers as peculiarly hideous.

One of the natives, a young man who had bisected his body
by a broad white line and dotted himself according to the latest
fashion on all parts of his body, came towards the dray, made
an obeisance to the white men, and said,—

"Dat your white man sit down dere?"

"Yes·" said Hugh.

"Tick—dat fellow" said Benbo, giving an explanation of
his meaning by signs, which Hugh translated into "sick."

"No."

"Drunk?"

"No."

Hugh noticed a brass plate with an inscription dangling
from the neck of the black fellow, and was regarding it attentively, when the wearer said—

"What name me?"

"BENBO, CHIEF OF THE WEIRABEE," said Hugh, reading it
on the brass plate.

"Yock-ki, clever, white man :—me Benbo :—me like white
man, and tea, and sugar, and bacca, and bread—all berry good.
What name you?" inquired Benbo of Hugh.

"Raymond."

"Eigh—Mitter Ramon—berry good name dat."

"Name you?" said Benbo, addressing Slinger.

"Slinger."

"Tclinger—Mitter Tclinger," stuttered Benbo in a vain
effort to pronounce the s, and producing a sound something

between a sneeze and a cough.—"No good name dat—Ramon berry good."*

"Ahoy! Weevel," said Slinger, arousing him from his nap by a smart rap on his back. Poor Weevel jumped on his legs as if he had been electrified. His face was almost as ugly as any of his sable contemplators. He saw nothing but the blacks grinning around him. Feeling assured that murder could be their only object, he seized on a portmanteau and laid about him with the valour of desperation.

"Yock-ki!—Berry drunk, white fellow," said the chief of the little party, as he retreated beyond the reach of Weevel and his weapon.

"Help!—Murder!!—Murder!!!" screeched Weevel:— "Raymond!—Slinger! Oh where are you?"

"Here we are," said Slinger, giving him a slight prick behind with a spear taken from the hands of a native. "What is the row?"

Oh I'm so glad to see you," said Weevel, recovering his courage, but panting with the exertion and excitement he had undergone.—"Fearful contest!—dreadful death!—Oh dear! Oh dear!—What a place to live in!—you fall asleep for a few moments, and when you awake find yourself at the mercy of— devils." This last word was pronounced sotto voce, as the bare possibility of the "devils" understanding so much English flashed across the discreet Weevel's mind.

In the fracas the looking-glass hat had fallen to the ground. It had not escaped the notice of the natives, who passed it

* The Australian natives having no sound of s in their language, find it almost impossible to overcome the pronunciation of it in another. If a Port Philip black fellow is told to say "split sixpence," he emits a spluttering sound resembling tplit tickpent—c

from one to the other, each making a grimace, and grinning into it as only Australian natives *can* grin.

"Oh!" groaned Weevel, growing very pale, "I'm wounded;" and he laid his hand tenderly upon the part;—"I remember feeling a stab in the heat of the conflict.—Oh dear!—Oh!"

"Where is he wounded?" said Hugh to Slinger.

"Oh, behind of course:" said Slinger, with a smile. "Weevel will never be hurt anywhere else, excepting by pure accident. I touched him up gently with a spear just now to bring him to his senses." Turning to Weevel, he said, "You are all right: you will never come to any harm as long as you can show such pluck as you have just done."

"Did I?" said Weevel;—"well, I think I did too:—rely upon it, Mr. Slinger, there's nothing like calmness in an emergency—nothing:" and as Weevel recovered from his fright he became proportionably valiant in words:—"I rather astonished them, I think, although single handed and unarmed.

A tribe of savages would have cowed an ordinary man: Eh Mr. Slinger?" But the difficulties of Mr. Weevel's position were not at an end, for although his person had escaped material injury, his trousers had been considerably damaged, and this new calamity disturbed him not a little,—"I can't get out another pair—what *am* I to do? and where is my hat?" Alas! it had disappeared, and so had the blacks.

Whilst Mr. Weevel was bemoaning his forlorn and helpless condition, a figure emerged from the scrub attired in the faded uniform of a Captain of Marines, its head covered with a hat marvellously like Mr. Weevel's. As it approached nearer, it was discovered to be Benbo the native, who, having been presented by some military colonist with the red rags, always took the earliest opportunity of appearing in them before strangers. He

H

approached with a majestic step, as if treading on the necks of emperors, and taking the hat from his head, which was literally plastered with fat and ornamented with kangaroos' teeth tied to the hair in little bunches, placed it respectfully upon that of its owner, and then, by way of fitting it properly, subjected him to the process known in England as "bonneting."— "Berry good hat," he said,—"black fellow only look—not teal." Weevel stood transfixed, whilst Hugh and Slinger were convulsed with laughter.

"What for you laugh?" said Benbo—"look at my coat," and he drew himself up with all the dignity of injured rank. He evidently expected some homage to be paid to his outward man; a failing not altogether peculiar to savages.

Having loaded the dray with their luggage and left the driver in charge, the party proceeded to the store, where Mr. Binns was ready to receive them. Mr. Weevel was introduced to the worthy merchant, but he was ill at ease, lest the unfortunate state of his trousers should be discovered. The three accompanied the proprietor of the store to a portion of it which was partitioned off, and where they were introduced to Mrs. Binns, a lady-like person, and one evidently unused to the kind of life she was then leading, she received the visitors kindly, apologised for the dearth of accommodation, and requested them to be seated on divers boxes and large cases with which the floor was covered. At every breeze, little jets of fine sand poured in with the sunshine, through the interstices of the weather-boards. Had there been no apertures for windows, the light, from a hundred imperfections in the woodwork, would have been sufficiently strong for most purposes. The store was deficient of any flooring boards, and the ground over which it was built was covered with a yellow sickly-looking grass very pleasant to walk on, and reminding Mr. Binns, as he assured his wife with a smile, of the old carpets they had left at home—in England. This was rather an unlucky allusion—it was received with a sigh. Against the sides of the store, hung upon stout nails, were sundry articles, all however coming under the category of useful—certainly not one was ornamental. There were several guns and pistols, a few native weapons, a sugar-bag cunningly suspended from the roof-tree, an arrangement very necessary but not altogether effectual, to protect its contents from the ravages of a small species of ant everywhere found in Australia. Several bags of flour were similarly disposed of to save them from the rats and other vermin. There was something so very homely and comfortable in the appearance presented by some sides of English bacon which hung aloft, that our friends instinctively paused to inspect them: they hung amidst the articles which surrounded them the *chef d'œuvres* of the collection.

Mr. Weevel was quite overcome as he regarded the spectacle before him, and the question arose in his mind whether the fate of an English pig was not preferable to that of a Port Philip colonist. How he wished he could be instantaneously transported to the land from whence that bacon came !

"Beautiful ! and English too," said Mr. Binns to Weevel, as he proceeded to cut some rashers for dinner—"I hope it will not grow rusty."

Mr. Weevel's comprehension of the properties of rust in bacon were, to say the least, original: observing the flitches were hung upon iron, he suggested that probably silver hooks instead would effectually prevent anything like rust.

"All this is very rough," said Mr. Binns, as he was preparing to cook a portion of their dinner; "but these are little matters we must put up with for a time. I shall be able to treat you better when my new store is finished, and when we can get a servant."

The dinner went off excellently, considering that the plates and drinking vessels were of tin, and the viands quite new to the guests.—Kangaroo-tail soup, &c. with rashers of bacon, formed the principal part of the fare; to which ample justice was done: bread, and a few—a very few, vegetables completed the repast.

"Mr. Weevel," said Mrs. Binns, "may I trouble you to drop that blind over the window—the sun annoys me."

To do this Mr. Weevel would have to turn his back upon the company, but he said "Yes—Oh yes—certainly Ma'am," and he edged away to the window.—Alas! the blind was hitched. "Get on the box," said Hugh, who was enjoying his confusion," then you can reach it." Up Mr. Weevel mounted, and the state of matters became quite perceptible. A suppressed titter announced the discovery of the catastrophe, in the midst of which the victim hurriedly descended from his elevated position, rushed over to Mr. Binns, and made a most heartrending appeal to his feelings—recounting the agony he had experienced, the state of mind he was now in, and lastly apologising for entering the presence of a lady in such a state. "Stuff and nonsense," said the host; "come with me and I'll rig you out in two minutes." They left the dining place for a short time, and when Mr. Weevel returned his extremities were enveloped in a garment about twice too large for him. "We are not so particular here Sir," said Mr. Binns, "and don't think much of a thing of that kind.—Don't make yourself at all uneasy," he said, as Mr. Weevel requested permission to get his boxes in from the dray, which was now arrived, for the purpose of obtaining some fresh clothing. The evening passed

pleasantly, and the emigrants obtained a good deal of information about the colony. In reply to an enquiry from Mr.
Binns what their intentions were, Mr. Weevel replied immediately, that he intended to get away from the colony as quickly
as possible. As Hugh and Slinger had no definite idea in
what branch of trade it was best to engage, they requested advice upon the subject. Mr. Binns recommended laying out a
portion of their small capital in the purchase of land in the
township, which was increasing in value daily. There would
be a good opportunity shortly as a Government sale of allot-
ments was advertised to take place; before leaving, Raymond
and Slinger requested Mr. Binns to purchase for them to the
extent of £200, provided he considered the price favorable.

As it was dark when the period arrived for them to leave,
their kind host accompanied them to the door of the most respectable Inn of which the settlement could boast. This was
a weather-boarded house of one story, containing four rooms
besides a bar. The place was crowded by rough-looking men
drinking and smoking. On looking into three of the rooms
they appeared quite full of people, and the smell of spirits and
tobacco pervaded the whole place. "O how dreadful!" said
Weevel:—"Oh dear!—Oh dear!"

Hugh shouted aloud for the waiter, who, in about ten minutes appeared smoking a short pipe, and announced his presence by exclaiming, "Now then what's the row?"

"Can we be accommodated with a private room?" Hugh
asked.

"Private, ha! ha! ha!—No: I should rayther say not.—
We don't keep private rooms—this is a public house."

"I see it is," said Hugh.

"You can have three shake-downs," continued the waiter
"if you want to stop here to night, we shall clear the house

soon, and I don't think more than two places are taken in the back sleeping apartment."

" What *is* a shake-down ? " said Hugh.

"A shake-down—why bless me, you are innocent ! " said the waiter.—" New chums, I spose : " and placing his hand familiarly on Hugh's shoulder, he led him into a room about eight feet square. The floor was spread from one end to the other with blankets. " There, my lad," said the condescending waiter, " that's a shake-down, and an uncommon comfortable kind of a thing too—when you are tired, mind—when you are tired."

Slinger and Weevel had now entered.—" What ! " exclaimed the latter, " are five men to sleep *there* ? " pointing to the ground.

" And why not ? " said the waiter—" it is comfortable coiling, I can tell you—you musn't be proud here."

" But I will pay for a separate bed," said Weevel, producing a sovereign.

" You can't have it for money—that's a fact," said the waiter ; and hearing more gold chinking in Weevel's pocket, he said, " I'll show one-pound notes agin your sovereigns with you any day." Mr. Weevel with dignity declined. " Money is plenty here," continued the waiter ;—" a man is nobody if he can't do *this* ; " and he put his hand in his pocket and produced a handful of notes as if they had been so much waste paper.

" I shouldn't wonder," whispered Slinger, " if they are all flash.—Let me see them again, Mr. Waiter, will you ? "

The waiter

> " Said nothing to indicate a doubt,
> But put his thumb upon his nose, and spread his fingers out,"

and left the room.

" That is a specimen I suppose," said Hugh, " of a colonial

servant—vastly familiar, impudent, and independent—and what a room too!"

"I declare," said Slinger, "it is worse than our cabin: we *had* a half-inch deal board between us there, but here ——" in bounced two rough-looking fellows smoking short black pipes, and talking and laughing most uproariously.

"New chums," said one in a more subdued tone of voice to the other.—"We are to be bedfellows to night, I suppose," he continued," turning round to the others.

"We don't know about that," said Hugh, somewhat out of temper.

"Well, if you arn't, strangers, will you just turn out of this, 'cause the house has been cleared of all but those who remain for the night: that's all—now out you go."

"I think," said Hugh, "as strangers, we might expect some slight show of civility from those who, from their appearance, must be used to this kind of life. I, for one, am not accustomed to be spoken so freely to."

"Nor I for another," said his partner "Raymond and Slinger for ever." At this stage of the proceedings Slinger edged up towards Hugh, whilst Weevel took up a position close by the door.

"Tell you what, strangers," said the first speaker, "I'm just as ready for a row as most men, but new chums ain't a fair match for me, they ain't up to the ways of the woods.—I didn't mean no offence; if I had, I shouldn't stop now. You see the bush arn't exactly the place to finish one's education in—it don't put on the polish: but it makes a man tough in the hide, I tell you, and rough in the skin, but it's all right beneath. We are like the stringy bark-trees of our forests, mortal rough to look at outside, but sound within—like them we can stand anything and thrive under it too. Now, if you *want* a row, say the word, I'm quite agreeable, if you don't, give us your hands,

I'm agreeable either way. Which shall it be, a jolly row or a jolly night of it? But I see you mean to shake down with us—that's right—we'll enjoy ourselves:" as a preliminary, the two bushmen commenced undressing and rolling up their several articles of clothing to serve for pillows. Their example was soon followed by the remainder of the party. Then they all laid down in such order as appeared most convenient, but Weevel still gave preference to the place nearest the door.

"There," said the former speaker, "now we are all snug, we'll have a song to begin with, and here goes 'Hurrah for the Bushman's Life, it is the best of any,'" and he was proceeding with his entertainment, when Weevel said innocently,

"I thought we came here to sleep."

"Did you?" said the singer.

"Yes," said Weevel.

"Well, then go to sleep, and never interrupt a good song," and he made a second attempt, and succeeded in bellowing through a lot of words, and a tune probably to the initiated, but certainly our travellers could not discover the least resemblance to one.

His companion now produced a black bottle and tendered it to Hugh who lay next him. He was going to take a sip, when a toast was demanded and as Hugh hesitated, one of the bushmen, taking the bottle from his hand, said, "now I'll give you something which I know you will drink, heartily—'Here's destruction to all our bedfellows but the humans.'"

"Bless me!" said Weevel—"mosquitoes?"

"No, worse than mosquitoes."

"What then—centipedes, scorpions, snakes?—it *must* be snakes said poor Weevel."

"No."

"What then? oh do tell."

"Soldiers, that's what they are. Why this is the haunted

room we arc in—there's a nest of 'em under the floor—nobody sleeps here who can help it. Look here," said he, "here's one." It was a red ant upwards of an inch in length—"that's a soldier, and he prods hard too," and applying his lighter pipe to the intruder, he scorched it to death. The bottle was now passed to Hugh, and after drinking the toast he passed it to his friends who followed his example. The bushmen smoked a pipe or two, gave some preliminary growls, and then they all fell asleep.

Hugh was soon roused by a sting, which made him start. He discovered the cause to be in the shape of a "soldier." Having destroyed it, he fell asleep, but was shortly awakened by Weevel's starting up and groaning. He saw this persecuted individual get out and proceed to dress himself in a fantastic fashion:—he put on his trousers and tied the legs of them round his ankles, then he put on his coat and fastened it tightly at the wrists.

"Why Weevel!" exclaimed Hugh, "what are you about?"

"I have been fearfully stung—I am being eaten alive!—what a shocking fate mine will be to record.—Oh dear!—Oh dear! I hope this contrivance will protect me," and he lay down again, but not to sleep. As soon as day dawned, he roused his party, and they disturbed the two bushmen, who lit a pipe apiece and got under the blankets again.

"Well mates," said one, "how about the sogers, eh?—but I see you are off. If any of you should ever be in the Westernport district, I shall be glad to see you at my station, so would my friend: we are neighbours, we only live four miles apart."

"You are very kind," said Hugh; "we may meet again: but you forget your names are unknown to us."

"I'm Ruffin," said one.

I

"And I'm Rugsby," said the other.

"Well, good morning, Ruffin and Rugsby," said Slinger, laughing, "you are a great deal better fellows than you look— Good bye—good bye," they said; "and thank you for the compliment."

The three having breakfasted, and perambulated the town for an hour or two, bethought them to go on board the "Big Ann," and say good bye to the captain and officers, as she sailed in a few days. Weevel had all his luggage taken to the boat in which they had made arrangements to go down to the bay. They pulled alongside the vessel and hailed her, but received no answer. Hugh clambered up the side by a rope which hung over, and not seeing any person astir, he knocked at the mate's cabin door, who appeared partly shaved.

"Ah my boys! how are you?" said Mr. Moriarty, in his hearty way.—"Come down to say good bye, eh?"

"Yes," said Hugh, "Slinger and I have; but we have brought you a passenger for England. Poor Mr. Weevel has seen enough of the colony to make him quite disgusted with it: but I thought you had left the ship to take care of herself— we could'nt see a soul moving."

"Why where are my men, then?" said the mate evidently startled:—"Turn out there, forred!—turn out you lazy skulks you!" This command met with no response. The mate went to the forecastle—returned in a minute, and exclaimed, "Every mother's son of 'em gone by jingo—bolted with their kits, and here we are without a single foremast man left, and none to be got here for love or money." It was too true, all the men had deserted in the night, leaving only the black cook behind them. They had taken with them their clothes in one of the ship's boats, and probably were by this time some miles in the country and engaged at exorbitant wages.

Weevel, however, tried to make an arrangement, whereby he was to live on board the ship all the time she remained in harbour, and then proceed in her to Calcutta, and from thence home. As there appears a prospect of losing sight of our friend, it may be as well to say, that however the Weevel species may thrive in a country like England, Australian air does not agree with them, and generally changes their habits, or drives them away. We must do Mr. Weevel the justice to state, that he returned the borrowed trousers to Mr. Binns, and appeared on the occasion dressed in the most elaborate manner; but we regret to record, that the effect he intended to have produced was quite lost, for on passing a gang of Government men* at work, he was hailed with such enquiries as—

"What were you transported for?"

"Did Government find you your toggery?"

We will not recount the adventures which befel the partners for the first two years spent in the colony, as during that period they seldom left the town, which had assumed a more compact and substantial appearance. The land which Mr. Binns had purchased for them at £20 the half acre allotment, had increased so greatly in value, that the same was now worth from £500 to £700, with its value still on the increase. The firm of Raymond and Co. made other good speculations, and so far all was prosperity.

One day about this time Slinger brought a packet for Hugh from the Post Office, containing information of the greatest importance. We have before said, Miss Leslie's property which was large, was in the hands of her guardian, Jarroll. By the

* Colonial for Convicts

letters now received, it appeared that this Jarroll had been detected in forging a will, and had been actually committed to take his trial for the crime. The evidence was said to be quite clear against him : and now came the part of the news which principally affected Hugh. For some months before the discovery of the "honest" lawyer's villany, Miss Leslie had been subjected to the persecutions of his son, and on complaining, was rather blamed than otherwise for not receiving his addresses. This made her most unhappy, and immediately on receiving intelligence of the suspicion which attached to her guardian, she sought and received the protection of old Mr. Raymond, with whom, so ran the letters, "she would reside for the present." Such was the state of matters in England according to Hugh's first advices. The next mail which arrived, contained a circumstantial account of Jarroll's trial, conviction, and sentence to transportation for life.

The deeds of Amy Leslie's property were not to be found, nor would he give any account of them. Upon this subject as well as all others he preserved a dogged silence.

CHAPTER VI.

SOME months afterwards, business in Melbourne proving dull, the two partners determined to purchase cattle and to go in search of a convenient station on which to run them. As the Westernport district had not been much explored at that time, they decided to proceed there. Accordingly an offer was made to the native Benbo to accompany them, the great inducement being that the party should carry plenty of tea, sugar, flour and tobacco.

"Yes" said Benbo "me go—me take my wife too—strong fellow my wife—carry ebbery ting—good fellow dat—no gammon my wife." A few days afterwards the journey was commenced. The two white men were dressed *á la* bush, each carried a kangaroo skin knapsack, one compartment of which contained a clean shirt, a small bag of flour, some tea, sugar, and tobacco, and a tin cup and plate; in the other was ammunition and the few articles of a bush toilet, namely, soap, a towel, and brush. On the top of each knapsack was buckled a thick blanket. Their guns were slung or carried in the hand as best suited the convenience of the bearer.

Benbo carried with him his native weapons, consisting of boumerangs, waddy or heavy club, a stone tomahawk, some long spears, and an instrument by which they are thrown, called a womera. A kangaroo skin bag was thrown over his left shoulder which contained them all, with the exception of the spears. His body was enveloped in an opossum skin rug, each skin being wrought in such a manner as to leave the whole as supple as if it had been tanned. His *lubra*, or wife, who was a short woman about eighteen years of age, was also dressed in the same garb. She had a full bag similar to her husband's on her back, which emulated a marine store in the diversity of its contents: there were wooden utensils for water, tin pots, an old saucepan, a chisel, a large lump of gum, a store of flour, and other provision for herself and husband (genuine from the mart of Raymond and Co.), six miserable puppy dogs, a half roasted opossum, and many other smaller but equally miscellaneous chattels; a little black child about two years old (whom Benbo had been commissioned by some of his tribe to take to its friends, vaguely supposed to be somewhere in the Westernport district) and whose bright little eyes and restless behaviour gave him the appearance of a small black dog on the *qui vive* over the treasures in the bag.

On reaching the opposite side of the Yarra, they found themselves amongst brick kilns and deep pits from whence clay had been dug; many of these pits were half full of stagnant water, and the bull frogs in them were keeping up a continual croaking. Little hovels rose here and there in which dwelt whole families, who were commencing their daily labour of making bricks. The party picked their way through the unhealthy territory, over which hung heavily a cloud of a leaden color, partly vapour and partly smoke, and pregnant with sickness and fever; on emerging from this swamp, the sun shone through a pure atmosphere, and a fresh breeze which was blowing, fanned the travellers as they moved onwards at a good pace, considering the unusual load each carried. Occasionally, after examining minutely the bark of a tree, Benbo would cast aside his cloak and weapons, with the exception of the tomahawk, and cutting notches in the bark, would mount and in a short time would be seen walking about upon the larger branches, prying into the decayed limbs in the hope of finding the opossum which his observation below had induced him to believe was an inhabitant of the tree. It was not often he was disappointed; and when having detected small portions of fur at the entrance of a cavity, he would insert a long twig, and hearing the opossum scrambling about inside, his merry laugh was worth listening to. He would then cut a hole at the extremity of the hollow part, all the time keeping up a continual chattering, addressing himself to the opossum, as yet unseen.—"Eigh! eigh! old 'possum (chop—chop—chop), you dere eh? (chop, &c.,) berry good; you wait a lilly bit (chop, &c.). Ah! Ah! me see him back (chop, &c.)—me make him door (chop, &c.). Now den,

where your tail, eh ? " and having seized it and twirled it round
rapidly several times, he would bring its head against a limb,
and as he watched its struggles, would continue, "Poor fellow,
neber mind ; me eat you by and by ; " and then apparently in
a great passion, " What ; you no die, eh? (whack—whack—
with the tomahawk) You ugly tief, me knock your eye out
(whack—whack). Oh! Ah! Dead, I beheb." If it were
not so, the fall from such a height sufficed to destroy life,
for he would let it drop from an elevation of perhaps seventy
or eighty feet, when his wife taking it, would add it to her
already extraordinary burden. This she sometimes cast upon the
ground, and with a small tomahawk, which she carried, would
cut into the root of a honeysuckle or wattle, and by means
of a small twig with a hook at the end, extract a large species of grub, from two to three inches in length, after regarding which for a moment, as a gourmand would a particularly
tit bit, she would give to the child or eat it herself.

"What a disgusting morsel!!!" says a sensitive reader.

Hast never eaten an oyster, Sir ?

About sunset, and after they had left Melbourne some miles
behind, Benbo expressed a wish to camp, and pointing to a hut
which could be just distinguished through the trees, said some
"good white fellows" lived there, who would give them food
and shelter for the night. " I think," said Slinger, "we will
economise our stores, and will only sleep in the open air when
we can't under a roof." " Agreed," said Hugh; and wishing
Benbo a good night, they advanced to the hut, and were received by several very fine kangaroo dogs (a breed between the
greyhound and bull-dog, noted for fleetness and strength), which
ran barking up to them, but were evidently not in a blood-
thirsty humour, for on Hugh speaking to one of them, it came
up and licked his hand.

" Halloo, strangers ! glad to see you," said a tall young man, as he opened the door.—" Our dogs are taught manners—they won't hurt you—they know better than to drive any one from our poor hut.—Such as it is, come in and welcome.—From town, I guess—What news ?"

" We are from town," replied Hugh, "and if there is any news, you'll find it in the Melbourne newspapers," and he produced several from his hat.

" Now then," said their entertainer, " sit down, we'll soon have something ready for you.—No grog to offer you, I'm sorry to say.—It wont keep in these parts, will it, Jim ?" he said, appealing to one of the other inmates.

" No," said Jim in return, " it wasn't made to keep, was it Tom ? "

" Of course not," replied Tom, who appeared to be the eldest of the family : " my brothers, gentlemen," he continued, with a sweep of his arm round the hut, " five on'em, and altho I say it, there aint a happier family in the country. We commenced our colonial edication with five year in Van Dieman's Land, and we're finishing it here. There's my brother Tom, there's Jack, Jim, and Bob; I'm Ned, and the youngest is little Jake (who was .about six feet out of his boots)—there; I haven't been so polite for a long time."

" Your hospitality and good feeling," said Hugh, is worth all the politeness in the world. But you have omitted to tell us your sirname.

" Did I ?—Martin :—a name well known in the Lincoln-shire fens :—but now take a tightner from that cold beef, you shall soon have some tea."

The two did ample justice to the fare which was set before them, whilst one of the brothers Martin, read the newspapers aloud for the edification of the others.

"I see," said Ned, "they are fighting again."

"Who?" asked Slinger.

"O! only the editors. When the *Gazette* was first published, the *Patriot* took to squabling, and getting the worst of
it, wound up a crushing leader, with a flourish something like
this—The editor of the Patriot regrets that he, 'a gentleman by
birth, rank, manners, and education,' should have condescended
to notice any remarks published in the columns of such a dirty
rag as the *Gazette*. Now it unfortunately happened, that
shortly afterwards the *Patriot*, who had been 'dining out,'
mistook the watch-house door for his own, and after repeated
applications, and a contest with one of the constables, he was
obligingly admitted, and the ensuing morning paid five shillings for the accommodation—the penalty for a clearly proved
charge of drunkenness being included under the same payment.
That was a glorious day for the Gazette, and the whole force of
the paper were at the police-office to triumph over the poor
Patriot in trouble. That was not the end of it, for when the
Gazette appeared next, one sheet was occupied with the following announcement—'Police News.—The Editor of the Patriot, 'a gentleman by birth, rank, manners, and education,' was
yesterday morning fined five shillings for DRUNKENNESS.'"

The party passed the evening in pleasant conversation, and
a shake-down being made, the brothers occupied it—a four-
post bedstead (literally; for the posts were in the original state
as brought in from the forest,) was allotted to the strangers.

Early the next morning Hugh and Slinger were roused by
Benbo, who had stalked into the hut, to the owners of which
he was well known. Having breakfasted, the travellers thanked their hospitable entertainers for their kindness, and proceeded on their way.

We do not propose to follow them through each day's jour-

K

ney, or to recount how they first bathed their hands in kangaroo blood, or what petty privations they submitted to when they were not fortunate in falling in with a bush hut. We lose sight of them till they arrive on the shores of the bay of Westerport, ten days after leaving Melbourne. Here it was considered advisable to dismiss their guide, as he was anxious to find some of his tribe, upon whose trail they had fallen. Benbo was accordingly told he could leave, and being presented with a little tobacco, took his departure, and he and his wife (whom he had named Kitty, as being more convenient and euphonious than her original designation, Montgurryburruckuck), were soon hidden by the trees.

"And now," said Slinger, "here we are dependent upon ourselves and a small pocket compass to point our way back again. I think we may venture to take a few days' shooting on the borders of the bay; there are lots of swans in a lagoon to the southward, so Benbo told me, and there is a cattle station beyond it, where we can get provisions if we run short."

"We may as well have all the fun we can, now we are out," chimed in Hugh, who had recovered his wonted spirits.

They travelled all that day, meeting with indifferent sport, as one swan and a duck were the only trophies they carried with them when they arrived in the evening at the bank of a creek, near which they determined to sleep.

"There's a snug-looking hollow tree," said Slinger, "and roomy, so we shall be comfortable enough;" and he advanced to the opening, but sprung back several paces, and raised his gun, as a man advanced from the hollow and cried, "stand!" after regarding them for a moment, he said, "What are you after here?"

"Anything which comes in the way," said Slinger.—"We are out for sport."

"Indeed!" said the man, somewhat incredulously. He was a tall and almost handsome fellow, of a wiry frame denoting great endurance. He had no hat on his head, but a piece of kangaroo skin, sewn in the shape of a skull cap, which served to protect it from the sun. His eyes were quick and roving, and his whole countenance, which was bronzed by exposure to the weather, wore a peculiarly keen expression. His language was good, and his address like that of one who had been used to a far different life than the one he appeared to be leading. He regarded every movement of the strangers with suspicion.

Hugh asked him how far he had travelled.

"Some distance," he answered; "my feet are sore and I am weary. I had retired to yonder tree to sleep."

"I am sorry we disturbed you," said Slinger, "you must sleep very tenderly."

A shade of suspicion flitted across the man's countenance, but it disappeared as quickly, as he said, "Yes: a man who travels much in the bush has need to—the blacks and bushrangers are very apt to put one into a sound sleep—the sleep of death, if he do not awake at a slight noise."

"Have you no shoes?" said Slinger, as he noticed his bare feet.

"None: my feet are hardened. I fear me, if it were not that nature is a good shoemaker, whose soles improve the more we wear them, I should be sadly at a loss. May I ask how far you have come, gentlemen?"

"From Melbourne."

"Was there any news abroad?"

"None of importance."

After a slight pause, Hugh said, "Perhaps you are hungry, will you share our supper with us?"

"Gladly," said the man eagerly; I havn't tasted bread for

weeks—days I mean," he said, on noticing the surprise with which his assertion was received; and the same suspicious glance was cast around him.

They soon kindled a fire and all seated themselves round it. Hugh produced some remains of a damper wrapped in a piece of a newspaper, and asked the stranger to fall to, who required no second invitation, but ate ravenously. After the meal was over the strange man was reading the paper when he started suddenly and put it into his knapsack, saying, it would be good for gun-wadding. Looking keenly at Hugh and Slinger, who were somewhat surprised at his excited manner, he asked where they intended to pass the night.

" I think there is room in the hollow tree for us all," said Slinger; but of course, as you were in possession, it remains to be decided whether you will allow of interlopers."

" Certainly, gentlemen; I shall be most happy to entertain you, although my accommodation is somewhat scanty: you must know that is a favourite tree of mine, in which I have slept many times of late. It has served me one good turn, I can tell you; besides protecting me from the wind and weather."

" Do you live in these woods, then?" said Slinger.

" I have of late: and the first night I arrived on the borders of yonder creek I saw this tree, and retired in it to sleep. I was awakened by a noise, and looking about me, could distinguish nothing strange, excepting what I took to be a dead stump standing in the ground where I had not noticed one before. Imputing this to my lack of observation I again laid down, but recollecting my gun was only loaded in one barrel, I roused myself again to charge it,—when the stump was gone. 'Now then,' I said to myself, 'for business;' for I knew I had blacks about me. Noiselessly loading my gun with a charge of shot and a ball on the top of it, I climbed up the hollow, taking my blanket with me and leaving my knapsack where I had been lying. I had got up as high as you see that hole, and from there surveyed the only part from whence the blacks could attack me. I had not been there long, when I noticed five dark spots on the ground, and although I could not decidedly say I saw them moving, yet the distance between them and me gradually decreased. I now felt certain it was the blacks, and could have shot two of them easily, but scarcely knew what their object might be, as I could distinguish no spears or other weapons. Taking off my belt I fastened my blanket to it, and lowering it with one hand, whilst I kept my face—which I had blackened with the charred wood inside the tree, lest they should distinguish it, as the moon shone brightly,—to the hole. I waited to see the result. The dark spots immediately, as I anticipated, became stationary, and rising like evil spirits from the earth, balanced each a spear for a moment, and then cast them at the blanket, which I let fall; they then advanced with a yell. I took as steady an aim as I ever did in my life, and fired both barrels, but *all* the savages dropped. 'That's three too many,' said I, as I loaded again. When next I looked from the hole I could only discover two bodies, one was quite still, the other was writhing in agony, it raised itself erect for a moment, and advancing with a howl, stumbled and fell, and did not move again. After waiting some time I was on the point of descending, when I thought I saw my blanket move; I looked again, and felt satisfied I was right; I pointed my gun to the ground, for I distinctly saw a spear pulled out of the blanket. I concluded from this that the other natives were short of weapons, so I jumped down; but before I could recover myself, was grasped from behind by a gigantic black fellow: I still how-

ever retained my gun: I clung to it with all the strength desperation gives, and inch by inch, in the struggle which ensued,
I at last got my finger on the trigger—it was at the right moment too, for a black fellow was advancing with a death cry on
his lips and flourishing a tomahawk; I managed to cock one
of the barrels and to point it at the black, and pulling the trigger
it exploded, and the black fellow who held me, let go his grip
on seeing his companion fall, which he did terribly wounded:
the tall fellow and his companion now made off through the
bush, but my blood being up, I took aim, and should have had
my long friend, but just then the fellow last shot turned over,
groaning in agony; so dropping my piece, thinking I had done
mischief enough for one night, I tumbled the two first shot
into the creek, for they were quite dead, and on returning to
the tree was surprised to find the other one gone. My gun
was all right, and I rambled about in the hope of finding him
again, but did not. I returned to my tree wondering what
could have become of him, and wondering on, fell asleep. I
awoke with a crushing blow and the sense of a heavy weight
upon my body, and the light of day just breaking, showed me it
was a human being. I gave myself up for lost, but grappled
with him and met with no resistance. A thrill passed through
me on feeling the flesh cold and clammy and the limbs rigid—
I grasped the body hard almost hoping to meet with some resistance, but met none:—I cast off the loathsome burthen, and
the dead man had done what, when living, with four others, he
had failed to do. I trembled with fear, and dared not for some
time remove the body, which was of the black who had so mysteriously disappeared. He must have managed to crawl up the
tree, and to prevent the flow of blood from his wound had filled
it up with stringey bark; there he must have died, and probably stuck in a piece of the hard timber which juts out and af-

fords a firm footing. I will point it out to you to morrow, and the mark of the spears. I shall never forget that night; but knowing the natives have a great dislike to remain in a neighbourhood where any of their tribe have died, I prefer to retain my tree rather than risk spending such another night. I often start in my sleep, and hear that groan, and feel the weight upon my chest, and have that fearful struggle with the dead. But, gentlemen, my yarn has been long enough for tired men, so let us collect some fire-wood and turn in."

A large fire was made up for the night, great logs were piled on it, and a cheerful blaze illuminated the landscape for some distance around. All but the stranger were soon wrapped in a sound slumber. He got up more than once and fed the fire, first bending his piercing glance into the impenetrable gloom of the forest : he made little noise, and Hugh and Slinger slept on. He lit some dead leaves to obtain a more brilliant light, drew from his knapsack the piece of newspaper which had occasioned his surprise, and read a portion of it attentively. It was to this effect—"Government Notice.—£200 reward. Whereas Richard Bayley,—alias the Scourge,—alias Hurricane Dick, a convict, escaped from a road gang, in the district of Menaroo, about two months since, by slipping his irons, and surprising the sentry, inflicted a blow upon his head of which he has since died; and whereas it is supposed he has organized a gang of bush-rangers and committed divers depredations. This is to give notice, that the above reward will be given to any free person or persons, not actually belonging to the gang, who shall take the said Richard Bayley,—alias the Scourge,— alias Hurricane Dick, dead or alive; and a reward of £100 and a free pardon will be given to any of his men who shall deliver him *alive* into the hands of justice."

"So much for that," he muttered, as he crushed the paper

in his hand and threw it in the fire.   As he watched its burning he continued, "Would that I could so easily destroy the records of my life; but it cannot be whilst memory lasts.—Richard Bayley," he said, apostrophising himself, for he was the notorious bush-ranger of whom tales were told enough to appal the stoutest heart,—"Necessity has made you live a brute's life, and it may be even yet you shall die a dog's death."   He spoke so loudly in his excitement, that the sleepers were disturbed.

"Halloo! Mate!" said Slinger, seeing him sitting up, " I thought I heard some one talking—I suppose 'twas fancy."

"No:" said Bayley: "not fancy:—I've been dreaming one of my cursed dreams again.—Good night," and Slinger soon slept as soundly as before.

"How do I know," muttered Bayley, looking round "but these very men are here to betray me?—Ah:" he exclaimed, as Hugh's head rolled off the knapsack which he was using as a pillow, "there may be information there," and he drew it towards him and examined the contents.   "No! No!" he said as he replaced it, "I do them an injustice, none but honest men with hearts at ease could enjoy such sleep as that;" and he leant over the sleepers and then regained his old position, saying, "When shall I sleep so again?—I who am put up for sale at a price—whose rest is a period of danger—who have been driven from bad to worse—whose enemies are all the world, for friends I have not one in whom to trust:" and he buried his face in his hands.   Presently he lay down and fell into a fitful slumber, occasionally starting and muttering strange unmeaning sentences.   Once he pronounced the name of " Jarroll," and shortly afterwards said, "the greatest rascal of them all."   Then he slept more quietly.

The morning sun shone in brilliancy, and nature's pearls glistened on the trees; for there had been a heavy fog, and

each leaf sparkled with its dew-drop. Ere the sleepers awoke
the sun's beams fell full upon their faces. A light breeze was
blowing up the creek, and as it sighed through the bush, set the
pendent leaves in a gentle motion, and shook from each tree and
shrub a mimic shower. Birds of every shade of plumage, flitted from spray to spray, and the insect world joined them in
their morning orisons. Parrots and paroquets continued a
subdued chattering as they flitted overhead; the notes of
lyre birds were heard from the distant hills, and nearer, the
delightful whistlings of the Australian magpies. Now and then
some black swans flew by with outstretched necks, and seeing
intruders on their domains, expressed surprise by shrill and varied trumpetings. The incessant chirping of myriads of locusts
lost its monotony, and with the ripling of the waves upon the
distant shore, blended every sound together so sweetly, that for
a time the travellers listened in admiration to the most delightful of all melody—the harmony of nature.

CHAPTER VII.

NUMBERLESS specimens of the Australian Flora bloomed at
their feet for which they knew no names but only that they
were beautiful—

> ————" Crimson buds, and white, and red,
> The very rainbow showers
> Had turned to blossoms where they fell,
> And strewed the earth with flowers "

On one hand, several varieties of heath clothed a sandy hillock,
whilst in an adjacent gully could be seen tree ferns rearing

L

their graceful forms and giving a tropical character to the scene.

"Is not this an earthly paradise?" said Hugh.

"No:" replied the stranger solemnly, "for it has been stained with human blood."

"I had forgotten that," said Hugh; "why did you call it to my mind? Methought it was a spot whereon a man could dwell for his life, willingly resigning all thoughts of the busy world, and hold converse with the God who made it.—It is most lovely—I never remember experiencing such a feeling of happiness as I do now."

"Happiness!" said the stranger; "I would that I could feel like you.—I did once, but years of ——" and here he burst into a rough laugh, and concluded "don't you think I preach well at times?"

"If you can regard a scene like this with indifference," said Hugh, "I do not envy you, and should be inclined to think that the life you appear to have led must have tended to destroy your nobler self."

"I have," said the other, looking up, "been used to such scenes of late years. I felt as you do once; but have wandered long in the woods, and it takes more violent excitements to move me now." He rose, and putting on his knapsack, said, "You have been so kind already to a stranger, that I am emboldened to ask a favor of you; will you spare a little of your flour and ammunition? for I intend leaving this part to day."

Hugh, taking his little store out, put it into his hand, saying, they should reach a station soon, belonging to a Mr. Dodge; "and here," he said, "is a little tobacco, powder, and shot." The stranger preferred bullets, if they could be spared, and received a few in addition. "You should have more," said Hugh, "but our stock is low."

"Thank you kindly, gentlemen," he said, as he shook their hands warmly; "if I had met with hearts like yours in times gone by, I should not now be what I am."

"And what are you?" said Slinger. "I see you have had much trouble, and it is possible we may be able to assist you further."

"You have asked me a plain question: had you addressed me so when we first met, we might not have been so friendly as we are; but your kindness and sympathy have done what iron gangs and lashes, and cruelties of which I dare not think, have been years in bringing to pass. My heart once more beats in unison with my fellow creatures.—you have taught me that all men are not oppressors. But, perhaps, even yet, when I tell you who I am, you too will despise—aye, or it may be, betray me. If you are not what you seem to be, honest and feeling men, in God's name let me go my way; but if your hearts do not belie your looks, seat yourselves and listen how I shall answer your question."

Hugh and Slinger sat themselves upon a fallen tree.

"Give me your words of honour (I have learnt colonial oaths are of no value,) that you will not mention this meeting or anything which may now transpire to any one, whilst such a revelation might tend to my injury."

"We give you our words of honour we will comply with your wishes," said Slinger and Hugh together—Slinger added in an under-tone to Hugh, "Romantic! aint it?"

"Enough:" said the stranger. "Have you ever heard of a fellow who leads bloodthirsty villains through the woods, himself the greatest wretch of them all, robbing unprotected stations and murdering in cold blood the unoffending inmates, destroying even little children, setting all laws at defiance, both human and divine—violating wives and sisters—marking his track with murder, fire, and devastation?—Have you ever heard of such a being?"

Before there was time for an answer, which Hugh and Slinger, who were speechless, certainly did not give, he sprung to his feet, and casting his gun from him, said,—

"The man whom such lies are spoken of is before you and in your power; work your wills upon him—he is desperate and prepared for everything that can happen:" he folded his arms and leant against the tree; his chest heaving with violent emotion. Neither of the friends spoke a word, and the bushman returned to his old position, and said, in a subdued voice, "I am Bayley, the notorious bushranger."

His listeners felt anything but comfortable at the information, for his name was the terror of the whole country.

"That very paper which I put in my knapsack yesterday contained a Government notice that £200 was set upon my head, dead or alive; and £100 and a free pardon to any of my band who will be base enough to sell me; and I fear," said he, "there was one, if not more, of those who lately joined me, that would most gladly do so. I heard of the notice fortunately, and left them all about a month ago, since which time I have performed alone a dreary journey through the trackless forests, over mountain ranges where no white man has ever set foot before; and through scrubs, in which, any, not driven by necessity as dire as mine, will never penetrate again. Gentlemen, what do you think of your companion now?"

This was what would be called in law a "leading question;" and Slinger in his outspoken way replied, "Well, I don't feel proud of your acquaintance," and he would have proceeded further, but on looking in the bushranger's face he saw enough there to induce him to be silent: it did not display anger, but there was a shade of deep misery upon it, which appealed to Slinger's humanity rather than to his courage.

The bushman continued,—" I have only shed blood to save my own life, and never then if I could avoid it. I know that for some time I and my band have been falsely accused of every depredation which has been committed; but that I have done much to regret, is too true. Let me give you a short history of myself during the last few years, and you will then be the better able to judge for yourselves. I am the son of an Irish gentleman. When young and inexperienced I was induced to join in an election row in a county town in Ireland, which ended in a serious fight between the soldiers and the people, who were flying, when the officer in command ordered another volley to be fired upon them. I was disgusted with this cruelty, and by example and exclamations rallied the people, who faced the soldiers, and although several fell, they beat them out of the town, unfortunately killing, with two others, the officer in command. A warrant was obtained against me as ringleader, and being tried, I was transported. I was sent to Van Dieman's Land, where it fell to my lot to be assigned to a master who had five years before been a bricklayer's labourer, but who, by his good fortune, aided with a great proportion of rascality, had amassed some money, and had actually been made a magistrate. This was the man I had to call master, and to obey his behests however tyrannical, without a word. I submitted to my lot for a time with patience; but one day, for a trifling thing, which he construed into an insult to the dignity of a colonial magistrate, he ordered me to be tied up and to receive three dozen lashes. He was surrounded by men who were bound to obey him as much as I was, and I was seized. I appealed to him in vain to spare me the degradation—to pause and consider whether he was not overstepping the bounds of the law and of humanity.

He told me to hold my jaw : 'it will be a satisfaction,' he said, 'to see the dignity of a colonial officer righted ; I shall remain and see the punishment, and if the scourger does not do his duty, he shall have three dozen himself.' Seeing he was inexorable, I broke from those who held me, dragged the scourge from the hands of the man who held it, and gave my unjust and cruel master the lashes he intended for me. None of the other convict servants would interfere, and I thrashed him until he was quite disfigured : his face was sliced with the thongs ; and had I got him now here before me, I would repeat the punishment, or perhaps do more ; for to this ill-bred hound, to his cruelty, his utter want of all consideration for others, his avarice and despicable hypocrisy, (for he pretended to be a Christian, and read prayers night and morning to his household, to which, by the bye, if any neglected attending, he would be ordered three dozen lashes), may I attribute all my sufferings and every crime I have committed since. Such was my master, better known as Black Robberson."

"Robberson! why what kind of a man was he?" said Hugh.

"Stout and coarse—he looked like what he is, a cowardly bully."

"The same who returned to the colony in our ship," said Slinger—"the very same."

"He had better have remained away," said the bushranger! "After I had treated him as I have told you, I was sent to Sydney to be worked in a chain-gang, from whence I escaped a short time ago, and have ever since been at large. In making this escape I should have been shot by a sentry, had I not struck him with my hand-cuffs : I fear he has since died of the blow. This is the only murder I ever committed, if it *must* be termed so ; but I have saved the lives of

many, and it is some consolation to me now. Tell me, gentlemen, were your preconceived notions of me correct?"

"I fear," said Slinger, "you are the victim of a heartless
and cruel system."

"My lads!" he said, again grasping their hands, "you two
are the first whites who have spoken a kind and friendly word
to me for years. I thank you for it from my soul." He stood
his gun against the tree, and seated himself by the fire. There
was no suspicion about him now: he had eased his mind of a
heavy burthen, and felt once again that he was with those of
his own species, who looked upon and treated him as a man,
though one stained with crime. He buried his face in his
hands and was silent for some time. He roused himself up at
last, and said, "It is possible you have heard some of my bad
deeds rendered ten times worse than reality. Let me tell you of
others of a different character, which you will probably never
hear from any other lips, but they are not the less true. At the
time I first took to the bush, and when the hue and cry was
strong after me, I went into Sydney in disguise to save a man I
had once known, who was condemned to death. I obtained
entrance to the jail at the risk of my own life, and supplied
him with a file—the next day he was to have been executed ·—
that night he escaped. On another occasion, my men had
taken two magistrates of the colony and clamoured for their
death I induced them to leave the matter unsettled until the
morning, when, as they were notoriously cruel to their convicts,
their fate would assuredly have been sealed. That night, after
exacting a promise that they would spare their convict servants
for the future, I cut the ropes which bound them, and they escaped. If I have killed one man accidentally to save my life, I
have spared twenty, even at the hazard of it. But the sun is
getting high, and it is time for me to go."

"But where are you going?"

"Any where to avoid falling into the hands of those who know me. Whatever may become of me," he said, lifting his skull-cap, "I shall ever remember the sympathy and kindness I have experienced at your hands. God bless you for it." As he spoke he moved away, and his figure was soon lost amongst the trees.

"I declare," said Slinger, as they commenced their day's journey, "I had no idea bushrangers were such confidential, penitential, and highly respectable characters. I fancy our acquaintance must be an exception to the general rule; but that won't save him—if taken he will not be spared."

"I fear not," said Hugh; "I have heard that colonial authorities know but of one remedy for crime—hanging."*

---

* An old colonist informed me that a chaplain of the Hobarton Jail, on one occasion, whilst scrutinising a gallows upon which ten bushrangers were to be executed, very coolly remarked, "Well, the beam appears to be rather short— nine men could hang there *comfortably*, but the tenth would crowd it." The storekeeper who had the contract for supplying the prisons, frequently used to be waited upon by the last functionary of the law, with an order something in this way, "rop and sop for sem," Reduced to plain English, it meant, "rope and soap for seven.

In 184— there was an unfortunate native executed for a murder, the committal of which he firmly denied to the last. He was an ignorant savage, made by law a British subject, and amenable to that law of which he had never heard, (still less understood,) condemned to be strangled. The law, when too late, provided him a chaplain to administer spiritual consolation in a language he could not understand, for he was from a tribe who lived far in the interior—many miles beyond where the Black Protectors ever penetrated, and speaking a dialect they had seldom heard. 'Twas well, perhaps, that the Bible was a sealed book to him, or he would have recoiled in disgust at the horrible mockery to the lessons of mercy and justice contained in its pages, presented in the punishment he was about to suffer. The end is soon told. the rev. chaplain attended him to the scaffold. When the prisoner reached the platform, he looked up and saw the awful preparations. the consoler was by his side. Whilst in gaol, the black having learned some broken English, the following specimen of gallows oratory took place —

They had scarcely reached the opposite side of a broad lagoon, which lay in their course, and put themselves in travelling trim, when a heavy thumping sound, which seemed to approach nearer and nearer, attracted their attention—

"Blacks," suggested Hugh.

"Kangaroos, I think," replied Slinger.

They hastened to secrete themselves amongst the branches
of a fallen tree which still retained its leaves, and were scarcely
secure, when Slinger whispered, "Here they come, the beauties
—look at 'em—one, two, three, four emus, as I live! Stand
by for the two biggest—you take the first shot." On they
came, making the ground resound with their heavy tread.—
"Now then—up guards and at 'em!" cried Slinger, as he fired
upon the advancing birds. Two were wounded: one of these
was quite disabled, but the other was not so much injured
but that he was rather a formidable antagonist at close quarters. "Don't waste any more powder and shot," said Hugh,
"I'll soon finish him," and laying his gun on the ground,
he approached the emu cautiously as it lay on its side. He
was in the act of seizing it, when, with a severe kick, he lay
doubled up upon the turf, and the bird struggled upon its
legs. In spite of a shot from Slinger's gun it was making off

" Where me go ? "

" To heaven, I hope."

" Where em ? "

" There," said the chaplain, pointing above

" Ki '—long way !!—plenty tea, and flour, and baccy dere ? "

" It is a good place," said the chaplain

The executioner then proceeded to pull a cap over his face, when the native
said, " What for you put him head in a bag, you dam black tief ? "

" Let us pray," said the chaplain. ¦

" No, me too dam frightened —Long way hem, eh ? " But before a
reply could be made, the native was in eternity, and the majesty of the law vindicated.

M

through the bush, when unexpected assistance appeared; for two fleet dogs passed in full chase and were soon alongside the wounded emu. One of the dogs being a young one, fell into the same error as Hugh, and was soon rendered *hors-de-combat* by a kick; the other dog, more experienced, still continued the chase, and in the excitement of it, Hugh soon forgot his accident. The old dog headed the bird, turned it, and running alongside, brought it again near the travellers. When both dog and bird were nearly exhausted, with a sudden spring the dog made a snap at the neck of the emu, and in a moment or two it lay dead.

The friends were congratulating themselves on their success, when they observed a human form slinking about amongst the trees, and evidently not caring to approach them nearer. "The owner of the dogs, I expect," said Slinger; "he must have his share of the spoil. Come on friend," shouted Slinger encouragingly, as he observed the stranger hesitated;—"come on; we are not cannibals."

"What the devil do you mean by trespassing on my ground?" roared the stranger.

This was a novel question to be propounded in a district where the only landmarks were provided by nature, such as a range of hills or a river, and both Hugh and Slinger could not refrain from a good laugh.

"Ah you may laugh," cried the stranger; "but I should jest like to know who you are—I jest should; and what you are doing in these parts."

"Now I'll tell you," said Slinger, "we are looking for a cattle run, and we want to find a Mr. Dodge's station."

"Oh! you want to beat up the quarters of that respectable old gentleman, do you?" said the stranger ironically; and after taking another scrutiny, he sidled up to the sportsmen.

"What did you take us for?" inquired Slinger of him—"bushrangers, eh!"

"Worse than that."

"No."

"Yes."

"Blacks?"

"Worse!—bailiffs. But you aint," said their new acquaintance, quite at his ease; "I know *that* breed too well. Now I'll be bound to be shot," said he, turning abruptly on Hugh, "if you ever fingered a writ."

"Well, I never did," said Hugh.

"I have,—hundreds," replied the stranger.

"You don't mean to say," interrupted Slinger, "that such creatures as bailiffs are ever to be found in this part of the world—does the law actually spread nets into this, the very fag end of creation?"

"Does it!—I *think* it does now and then; but it never makes much of a haul," replied the stranger, with a chuckle.—"I've known as many as two men a month wanting to meet with a friend of mine who lives about here—he never was to be met with, which was unfortunate, for they used to come all the way from the supreme court in Melbourne, and always on particular business too: at length old Dodge, for he is the friend I am speaking of, gave 'em so many specimens of his inventive genius, that for many months they have ceased troubling him."

The sportsmen now informed their new acquaintance that they were anxious to reach this Dodge's station before night, in order to procure flour, for their stock was well nigh exhausted.

"Then you are not after old Dodge himself, eh?—only his flour?"

"We should be most happy to make his acquaintance. I presume, from your description, he must be a character," said Hugh.

"Character! Eh! You must not ask the Melbourne sharks for it: if you do, you will hear of one not worth having. Now let's shoulder the emus; there's lots of oil in these fellows good for bruises, sprains, rheumatism, lumbago, and all that. I have a boat in a creek yonder, and shall be happy to take you to Dodge's station—'tis on the borders of the bay of Western-port."

"Perhaps," said Slinger, "this Dodge will not receive us very civilly: he might make the same mistake you did, and treat us as bailiffs; although, I must say, I should not feel flattered by his doing so."

"No he wont," said the stranger; "I can answer for that;" and he called his dogs to him and examined the one which had been hurt in the late affray.

They then set off for the creek, which was not far, carrying the birds between them. The stranger dragged his boat out of the mangroves which lined the muddy banks, and deposited the spoil in the stern sheets, launched her over the mud into the water, and they drifted slowly down.

"To whom are we indebted for this kindness?" Hugh asked.

"To that respectable gentleman I spoke of—old Dodge himself—He is your humble servant.—Strangers, allow me to introduce to you Giles Dodge—squatter—an outlaw (that means out of the reach of the law, you know,)—the will-o'-the-wisp of lawyers—the terror of bailiffs—and as good a rifle shot as any in these parts; who can sneak a kangaroo or a bailiff with any man in the settlement—if he can't may I be darned." What the process of darning might mean was not probably within the comprehension of his listeners; but as he shut one eye in an eccentric manner and threw his face into strange contortions, the reader may conclude that it must have signified something very dreadful indeed.

CHAPTER VIII.

Mr. Dodge was about forty years of age, although he looked ten years older; he stood six feet in his mocassins; as for
boots or shoes, his feet had long been deficient of those luxuries.
He was spare and wiry, his features sharp, decided, and angular;
his nose aquiline and slightly drooping at the point; his deep-
set eyes were grey and piercing. His invariable dress was a
blue flannel shirt, a pair of loose canvass trousers, which had
once been white, but were something of the color of ma-
hogany, with a fine polish about the knees, they were studded
with stains of blood and a few burnt holes. Round his waist
was a broad belt fastened with a massive silver buckle: suspended from the belt was a knife, a pouch made from the skin
of a platybus,* containing a pipe, tobacco, and a tinder-box.
His head was covered by a broad-brimmed Manilla hat, such
as a quaker might have envied. His beard was long and straggling, but the moustache which mingled with it was unexcep-
tionable. He was altogether a strange mortal even for the
bush, but he was a universal favorite, and a welcome guest
wherever and whenever he appeared.

Dodge's father was an English gentleman, and he himself
might have been one, had he not, imbued with the spirit of adventure, left his home too early in life to render permanent and
decided the advantages derivable from his position. Through the
rust of bush habits and feelings, which had grown about him
during many years spent in the woods, there were still to be discovered traits which clearly distinguished him from ordinary
bushmen. The misfortunes which beset him he accounted for,

* Ornathorencus paradoxus.

from the fact of his never, in all his life, being able to pay a debt until it had been doubled by law expenses. He generally used to know when any suspicious-looking strangers were *en route* to Westernport through some friends who occupied stations upon the road, and (as he significantly expressed himself,) "got time to clear out," if he surmised, as was often really the case, that the parties were bent on serving him with a writ, a summons, or on transacting similar law business. Many a time, after due deliberation, and generally at the proper season, Dodge would be seen leaving his station, mounted on his faithful steed with a tether rope neatly coiled upon its neck, and followed by his dogs; a blanket strapped on the top of a well-filled kangaroo-skin knapsack, indicated that the wary old fellow had been signalised "not to be at home;" and if any doubt yet remained, it would be entirely removed on finding that, previous to leaving, he collected all his cattle and drove them leisurely through a mountain gorge opening into some fine pasture land, the existence of which was only known by a few. Many were the desperate straits to which he had been reduced, but his genius as often triumphed.

Whilst the party sailed down the creek, the amusing Mr. Dodge recounted several of his hair-breadth 'scapes. The following he told with great gusto, but we must take leave to present it to the reader in our own way.——

An advertisement appeared in the Melbourne papers as follows:—"If Mr. Giles Dodge, squatter, of Westernport, or elsewhere, will wait upon J. Nailem, Esq., Solicitor, Melbourne, he will hear of something to his advantage. N.B. The melancholy duty which devolves upon the advertiser, in having to make known to Mr. Dodge his severe bereavement in the demise of a near relative, will, he trusts, be somewhat mitigated by further intelligence which he is prepared to communicate." A newspaper containing the above reached Mr. Dodge in the course of a month or two from publication. Concluding that his father was the "near relative" therein alluded to, and that a remittance was the result of his death, he set off without delay for town, intending, as he said, "to square up his accounts and to turn over a new leaf." In due course Dodge found himself thread-ing the intricacies of the "brick-fields"* which stretch along on the banks of the Yarra opposite Melbourne, and crossing the river in the punt, he rode boldly into the town. After refreshing his horse and himself—the horse was always the first thought of—Dodge went boldly in quest of the solicitor; but he went on horseback, for he knew that his steed "Charley," who had borne him some thousands of miles, would not fail him at a pinch. He found Mr. Nailem's office without much difficulty: it was a weather-boarded building of one story. Leaving his horse to graze near, he was shewn inside, and was presently waited on by the redoubtable Mr. Nailem. Dodge made known his name and business.

"And so you are Mr. Giles Dodge of Westernport, are you, Sir?" inquired the lawyer.

"I am," said Dodge. "You have unpleasant news to com-municate."

"Very," said the other, with a grim smile; which did not es-cape Dodge's notice, for he could not comprehend how it could presage bad news; besides he detected a stifled laugh from the clerks' office. "I have something which will surprise you; and he turned over a pile of papers which lay on a desk, pre-sently singling out one, he dallied with it for a short time, still conversing with Dodge, on whose mind flashed a suspicion that

---

* According to late accounts "the Brick-fields" are covered with the tents of newly arrived emigrants

foul play was intended. He determined to be on the *qui-vive*, as he was now completely in a trap.

"It is my painful duty," said the lawyer, advancing, and opening the document, which at a glance Dodge knew was a writ, "to arrest you in the —"

"O don't!" said Dodge, falling on his knees, but very near the door;—"forgive me this once; I will never attempt to be dishonest again. I will confess all.—I saw the advertisement, and being something like Mr. Dodge, I thought, just for a joke, I'd answer it—that's all.—Don't apprehend me—consider my wife and little ones."

"To think," said Dodge, as he reached this part of his narrative,—"to think of penetrating a lawyer's heart with a plea, for wives and little ones—ha! ha!"

"How!—What?" cried the lawyer, "not Dodge?—you *are* Dodge."

"I wish I was," said that personage mournfully, "for I heard his father was dead and that you had some money for him, and that was what the advertisement meant, and I came here for a joke."

"Joke!" cried the lawyer; "how dare you trifle with the law this way?" The attorney paused for a moment, and calling his clerk by name, said, as he appeared, "You heard what this fellow said;" and turning to Dodge, "What if I detain you—have you taken in charge, tried and transported—that would be a pretty ending to your *joke*.—Eh?" and then, after a pause he added, as a sudden thought struck him, "Do you know Dodge?"

"I did once—can't say whether I should just now, you've frightened me so."

"Does he know you?"

"I'm not sure."

The lawyer took one or two short turns, and Dodge eyed the door. Turning abruptly, the lawyer asked,

" Were you ever at Dodge's station? "

" Yes."

" You know your road there? "

" I think I might find it."

" Well, then," said the lawyer, " you shall hear no more of this joke of your's (by the bye, it is a transportable one you know), provided you'll do me a little service.—Mr. Smith," he said, turning to his clerk, " you are aware that this man has confessed that he came here to personate Giles Dodge, and intending to obtain money under false pretences? " As if Dodge's previous confession was not clear enough, he stammered out, despondingly, " I did—but only in a joke though." "A jury would show you " the lawyer remarked, " where the point of it lay,—but enough of this: do you consent to help and arrest Giles Dodge or not? "

" I hope he has not been doing wrong," said Dodge,— " not branding another man's cattle, nor anything of that kind, has he? "

" Never mind what he has been doing: I rather think we shall do him yet," he said, rubbing his hands violently.

" I rather think *not*," Dodge said—to himself.

The lawyer left his office for a minute, laying the writ on his desk. During his absence Dodge satisfied himself it was intended for him, and substituted for it another which was at hand. He had scarcely done so, and was nearly choking with laughter, when the lawyer returned. Seeing Dodge's face red, he said, " You have been drinking: I see you have—you had better be careful what you are about, or you will wear the ruffles yet—you are quite aware you are in my power." Of course

N

Dodge *was* quite aware of it, in fact he was much clearer on that point than the lawyer himself.

He continued, "Now all you have to do is to accompany the person who will be here presently, show him the nearest way to Dodge's, lend him all the aid you can, and if the capture is made within the week I will make you a handsome present—there! and you shall hear no more of your '*joke.*'"

"Thank you kindly," said Dodge, and he breathed freely once more.

Mr. Grabley, the bailiff, soon arrived, and Dodge prepared himself for his new duties. He examined his horse's feet, took an extra pull upon his saddle-girths, and looked to his spurs.

"Mr. Grabley is waiting, Sir," said a voice from the "clerk's office" by day, and bedroom at night.

The lawyer having fully explained to the bailiff the business to be transacted, accompanied him to the door, where Dodge was already in his saddle and attentively observing the bad points in Mr. Grabley's horse. As that functionary appeared, he observed to him, rather abruptly, "That's a screw, if *I* ever saw one."

"Well, he is rather stiff to day," said Grabley, "but he did forty miles yesterday: so we must ride easy."

"Slow and sure," suggested Dodge.

They were now ready to start upon the journey. The lawyer had given his parting directions; when, turning to Dodge, he said, "By the bye, my fine fellow, I want your name, if you please."

"My name," said Dodge, "ah—yes—to be sure! My name is—have you a pencil about you? write it, you *might* forget it.—Are you ready?"

The lawyer *was* ready.

"Now then," said Dodge, as he seated himself firmly on his saddle and mentally noted the probable speed of Mr. Grabley's horse; "sharpen your pencil and begin with a D: have you got that down?—O: got it?—D—G—E." Mr. Nailem's eyes opened very widely as he ended also with a D.—

"Dodge!" stuttered Mr. Nailem—"Arrest him Grabley."

Mr. Grabley produced the writ, and was about executing it, when Dodge suggested, in a quiet and collected manner, the propriety of examining it further. On doing so, the bailiff found, to his dismay, that he had been provided with a wrong one. Dodge was in his glory. The lawyer was beaten on his own ground. Turning sharply on the bailiff, who was not recovered from his surprise, Dodge dealt him a smart blow which threw him from his saddle, and then putting spurs to his horse he rode through the town at full speed, shouting, at the top of his voice, "Whoo-oop—whoo-oop—hurra!—I'll show you the road to Westernport!—hurra!"

With several such anecdotes Dodge wiled away the time, they were drifting down the creek, and so pleasantly too, that they found themselves in the bay of Westernport much sooner than they expected. it was a large expanse of water, and the tide had not long turned, but even then a few of the mudbanks, which render its navigation so difficult, could be distinguished. The low shores of French Island just rose above the level of the flats, whilst further inland stood some hills capped with high trees. Several dense columns of smoke mounted up near the shore, which attracted the attention of the boat's crew. "The mangrove burners are lighting up fresh fires, I see," said Dodge; "there are two living over there, they are the only inhabitants on the island. I put in there the other day for water, and was surprised to find a notice stuck up on a post at the entrance of the hut to the following effect.

"If any boat's crew puts in, it is particularly requested they will immediately search the bay to the northward for a boat, supposed to be capsized, and the person who sailed in her drowned." There was also a blanket hoisted on a pole as a signal of distress.

"Well, off I started immediately, but could get no news of the boat or her passenger. On returning again to the hut I found the remaining inhabitant, the last man, who informed me he had been three days in suspense, as he had seen the boat in which his late companion had sailed capsized about a mile from the island, and shortly afterwards fancied he saw her bottom up We immediately sailed together for the station to which the supposed sufferer was bound, and had scarcely entered the creek, when we saw his boat all right, and soon afterwards the dead man himself with a pipe in his mouth. It appeared that not being much of a boatman, he had allowed his only sail to be blown away in a squall, and after drifting about some hours, had fortunately made the creek. I've had a few adventures on that island myself," said Dodge,—"what with snakes, and rats, and fires, and last, not least, bailiffs—Oh they are rum cattle, they are!"

"Do spin another yarn," said Slinger, who was mightily delighted with Mr. Dodge and his narrations.

"Well, lads, I will; what shall it be about?"

"Oh, anything interesting."

"I've told you how I served a bum in the town; now you shall hear how I treat 'em when I catch 'em in the bush. About six months ago a fellow came down from town to serve me with a writ, but although I am pretty well known by name, there are few of the law gentry who have ever caught sight of me· and those who have, never express any great desire, that ever I heard of, to improve the acquaintance. Information once

reached me that a limb of the law was working down my road.
Three days after he arrived in my neighbourhood. I met
him about a mile from my station—much too near to be
pleasant. He was like every other bailiff you may have seen—
there's an unmistakeable likeness in all the breed—they don't
alter much anywhere. He looked as if he could have cut a
pocket out for the sake of the rag; but as I have not worn
pockets for many years, I had no fear on that score. "Mr.
Giles Dodge, I believe," he said, coming close alongside me;
but this was all guess-work, for I had never seen the man
before in my life."

"Well," said I, "you are complimentary, stranger, this
morning; and do you really take me for that notorious old
scoundrel, do you? Why, do you know I wouldn't like
to bear his name, much more his character,—there now;" and
I turned away highly offended.

"I beg your pardon," said the man, for the mistake; "but
may be, you can just pint out to me the way to his station.
—The fact is, I've a got a little matter here for him, and I'll
stan suffin ansom if you'll put me on his trail;" and he winked
his eye knowingly.

"There, now," said I, "now I *can* help you, and pay the
old blackguard out, for a grudge I owe him. I was at his
station this morning after some of my strayed cattle, when I
heard he was gone over to the island shooting swans. I have
a boat over in the creek yonder, in which I'll take you across,
and you may nab him as easily as you could me."

" Ha!—Ha !—Ha ! " laughed the man; "capital.—Thank
ye—thank ye: I'll stan suffin ansom, as I said before, and
give you grace if ever I have anything like this for you," and
he produced a suspicious-looking document from his pocket.

"So he got into this same little boat, and I paddled him

across the bay, and arriving in the latitude of one of the deepest mud-flats I know (and, let me tell you, in these parts they are pretty considerably pappy,) "and now," said I, running the boat aground upon the softest part of it, "you must get out on this bank and walk ashore to the hut you see yonder, where you will probably find him; if not, wait, and he will soon appear."

"But this ground don't look hard," said he.

"Not just on this spot, perhaps, but a good jump from the boat will carry you to the hard part, and then you will be all right."

"But I don't see his boat."

"Oh no : old Dodge is wide awake; he always hides it in the mangroves."

"Oh—does he?" said the bailiff, as he was swinging his arms backwards and forwards to procure the desired impetus that was to propel him to a firm footing. Had his efforts been successful, it would have been something extraordinary, for the mud-flat only terminated at the beach, which was full a quarter of a mile off.

"Had my passenger," continued Dodge, "looked round at this moment, he would have smelt a rat, for I was fearful of hurting myself, such were my violent efforts to restrain laughing aloud. He made the spring, and—and, Ha!—I never can tell this part of my story for laughing,—and he was up to his waist in a quicksand. The fellow stuck fast and was petrified with rage. After a flounder or two, reminding me of a sting-ray left ashore by the tide, he partially recovered his senses, and slowly dragged himself towards the boat, which I pushed into deeper water. He was wading after her when I said 'Do you see that shark's fluke there above the surface? Your being of the same species is no protection for you, for they eat each other, and I shouldn't wonder but they prefer a land-

shark for a change; take my advice, get ashore as soon as
you can and dry yourself in the sun before evening, because
it strikes me as likely that you wont get off the island for a day or
two. I'm Dodge. When quite convenient to me a boat will be at
the beach by the hut, and if you behave civilly, you will be taken
on board, not else; let this lenient punishment act as a lesson
upon you and the likes of you never to come to Westernport
again after Old Dodge, or he will have recourse to severer mea-
sures than he has done in your case. Do you hear what I am
saying?'

"The poor bailiff had now regained the mud flat, and I
pulled the boat near him again, when he said 'Do not leave me
here alone, dear Mr. Dodge, I will destroy the writ, I will do
anything, O don't,—don't, I will stan suffin ansom, I will
indeed, only take me back again.' 'Prisoner on the mud,' said
I impressively, 'do you think to tamper with me?—No! I'm
a determined man, I am; it is a duty I owe to myself and to
my friends at Westernport, to make an example of you; had I
gone the entire animal, I should perhaps have given you a
week of it, but in consideration of this being your first offence, I have allowed mercy to outweigh justice.' Here the ungrateful rascal had the audacity to cry out for more mercy. 'Why
you greedy beast,' said I, 'if you don't stop that dreadful noise,
I shall have to give you a week yet. Now, I said, if you wish
your sentence to be reconsidered, tell me how many writs you
have for Westernport men?'

"Two Sir," he whimpered, besides your'n."

" Will you oblige me," said I, " by trying if they will float,
just chuck 'em into the tide-way," and he did so. "All right,"
said I; " now get ashore the cleanest way—be as quick as you
can, for the tide is making, and don't stop to thank me for my
forbearance.—bye—bye;" and amidst a volley of entreaties

and curses, I sailed from the island.   Not a single writ has
been heard of since in the Westernport district.

"They call me," said old Dodge, evidently highly gratified
at the cognomen, "the Bum Perisher; and I am too; for although the last fellow down failed to catch me, he caught a
fever which he took back with him, and it killed him in a fort-
night.   I have thought since whether I didn't leave him *one*
night too long on the island; but whether or not, he was only
a bailiff."

The two friends could not quite reconcile the extraordinary
nonchalance Dodge exhibited at the poor fellow's fate with the
apparent goodness of his disposition; but the reader must consider that Dodge looked on bailiffs as his natural enemies, and
treated them accordingly.—Expecting no quarter himself, he
gave none.

"If the breeze holds," said Dodge, "we shall soon be home,
for near to the shore stands my hospitable mansion—that is to
say, when I have anything upon which to display hospitality, as
it fortunately happens just now, unless the rats have bored into
my flour-bag, and the wild dogs got at my beef-barrel.   Now I
dare say after all I have told you, you think me a queer fish—
indeed, I am disposed to think so myself sometimes."

"I've been all sorts of things.   I was once," he continued,
"a midshipman—and on getting a little property of my own
(I didn't save it out of my pay," he said impressively), "I cut
the water for the woods, and buried myself for a time in the
forests of one of the western states of America; but the Yan-
kees were too slow for me, so I sold off all my traps, and one
fine morning turned up in the salubrious colony of Australia
Felix   My present residence is a building in the semi-demi-sa-
vage style, designed and executed by myself.   It is surrounded
by park-like lands, on which great mobs of kangaroos roam in

liberty, affording me intense sport, and occasionally a dinner. Forty-eight stately cattle and my old horse 'Charley,' (how he can go !) are the only remnants of the large herds once owned by the noble proprietor."

CHAPTER IX.

As they neared the "hospitable mansion," the style of its architecture became fully developed. It was a square building of one story. The four walls were raised some seven feet from the ground, and were composed of split slabs set upright about three inches in thickness, and many of them standing at least three inches apart. Dodge explained that he was particularly fond of air, and therefore he was rather glad that the green timber had shrunk considerably. The hut was roofed with broad sheets of stringey bark lapped one over the other, and this perhaps was the most efficient work of the whole. The chimney, which occupied a considerable space, was built up with mud and turf. There was an apology for a window, which was stuffed up with flour-bags and dried grass; but the door and its hinges was a triumph of inventive skill, of which Dodge was justly proud.

After relating the difficulties which had beset his attempt at building, heightened by the want of several articles which are generally held to be indispensable (one constant source of annoyance was a great scarcity of nails), Dodge came to the matter of the hinges.—"I had a boy," he said, "who helped me with the cattle.—Oh! he was a boy.—I called him 'the Gorger:' first, because he was in doubt about his own name; and secondly, because, although only a boy in years, he

o

had the appetite (but he had the heart too) of a man   Well, the Gorger and I, after putting up the hut as you see it, were considerably bothered about a substitute for door-hinges. 'Nail up strips of bullock's hide to the door and to the wall,' suggested the Gorger.   But where are the nails, Gorger?—Some old fellow once said, if he could find a resting place for his lever he would move the world.—Find me the nails, Gorger, and I will hang the door. Try again Gorger. And the Gorger thought and thought until he grew hungry, when he set to work upon a piece of beef and damper, and then fell asleep. Happening to have a half bottle of rum in store, I took it out of plant (how fond Gorger was of rum to be sure!) and after a glass or two I felt as if I was getting nearer the solution of the problem.   The bottle at last stood before me in all its hideous emptiness:—in an attempt to drain a few last drops from it, I turned its bottom upwards.   One hinge was before me— the problem was worked.   So I woke the Gorger, D'ye see the hollow in the bottom of this bottle?—Well, that's a hinge—rummage out another bottle—that's a pair of hinges: put one bottle in the ground, bottom upwards, another in the slab above the door, bottom downwards; fix the ends of the post the door is built on into the hollows, and the thing is done. 'Mind the bottles are empty, guvnor,' said the Gorger. Leave me alone for that, Gorger, said I.   And now we are on such an interesting subject as the bottle, I mean to talk a bit—I hate a man who is eternally abusing it. Now there are two ways of doing this; one is by getting drunk on its contents and breaking heads with it, and the other by an indiscriminate condemnation of all liquoring. And baccy too—fancy a bushman abstaining from baccy!—Ridiculous. Leave him his baccy and he is not destitute:—it is often his substitute for every other comfort.   Baccy and the bottle are the first signs of civilization : they work their way long before every thing else. When a white man passes through the bush, he can't leave a church, a theatre, nor a gallows behind him (all marks of civilization in their way), but he very likely smashes a bottle or a pipe, and whoever follows after, knows, by these tokens, that he is treading in the steps of the white man. Ah! the bottle has noble uses," he said with a smile as he glanced towards the door-post of his hut.

"Yoic! old lass! yoic! old girl!" he shouted as a fine kangaroo dog came bounding down to the water's edge to welcome her master. The dog gave signs of uneasiness by an occasional growl, which, although unnoticed by Hugh and Slinger, was not so by Dodge.

"Do you see my old Lady there?" he said, looking after his dog attentively; "there's something in the wind."

"Why you are not married, are you, Mr. Dodge?" inquired Slinger.

"Married!" said Dodge, "Married!—ha!—ha!—Married!!—ha!—ha!——ha!—Old Dodge married!—ho!—ho! ho!—Dodge domesticated!!! Well, that *is* good. When I was a ladling," he continued, as well as he could speak for laughing, "a gipsy once told me I should be wedded to a dark lady with beautiful teeth and black hair. She must have imagined me just situated as I happen to be, for *I am* visited occasionally by some very dark ladies, and gentlemen too; and who knows," said Dodge, "but Miss Dulkey-bulkey, 'the Big Smutty Pot,' or, 'the Dowager Lady Yaller-nibberon,' otherwise, 'The Warm Blanket,' may not captivate me.—Married! no, no. I was talking of my dog 'Lady;' and she, dear old creeter, is talking to me. You don't understand her, but I do: and she's letting me know as plainly—as plainly as I see that fellow on the opposite side of the creek to my hut to keep a look out for squalls; and I will too. Humph!" he said, after a scrutiny, "I don't like his cut, for he has not altogether the bearing of a bushman, though he's rigged like one."

As the boat neared the landing-place, the stranger saluted them, and inquired, in a bland voice, "Is this Mr. Dodge's station?"

"Too polite," whispered Dodge to Slinger; and in a higher tone—"Dodge's station! O no: Dodge's station is higher up the creek by a good three miles, and I wish 'twas further off."

"How so?" inquired the stranger.

"Because he's a queer neighbour, and we can't agree. I'm right again," whispered Dodge to Slinger; "I'm sure its one of my old friends."

After landing his passengers, Dodge pulled his boat boldly across, and after a short conversation with the stranger, he agreed to accompany him on his way; first, however, re-crossing to tell his friends to help themselves to anything they could find in the hut, and to make themselves quite at home: "and now," he said, "for the present, good bye; I shall return about sun-set, after I have shown this gentleman a little of the interior."

Dodge again joined the stranger, and fastening his boat to a mangrove tree, they wended their way up the banks of the creek through an occasional scrub or swamp. By one of those stories for which Dodge was never at a loss, he drew from the stranger the purport of his business: it was neither more nor less than the serving a writ upon Dodge, "for which I shall get well paid," said the bailiff,—"out," muttered Dodge.

They were skirting an extensive tract overgrown with dwarf trees matted together with the thread-like fibres of the native vine, when Dodge said, "Come, shove along, we must get through this."

"Dear me," said the man, "I declare it looks impossible: we can't do it."

"Try," observed Dodge dryly, "Dodge's is a most difficult station to get at, I can tell you. Come on," he said, as he pushed his way into the scrub, "follow me." The bailiff stumbled after Dodge, tearing his clothes and flesh at every step.

"Look out for the snakes," said Dodge, after they had been in the scrub some time, "the place swarms with 'em, and such monsters too, nine and ten feet long, and as deadly as death's own darts."

"Let us go back," said the bailiff, alarmed.

"Oh no," replied Dodge, "never say die; besides, you are to be well paid too." This reminder somewhat rallied the sinking spirits of the poor bailiff, but in a short time he evinced unquestionable signs of exhaustion. "The wild blacks have a strange partiality for this scrub," continued Dodge; "every now and then they make away with a stock-keeper for me. The last poor fellow they caught of mine was a sad case. They roasted him alive, and scraped his flesh from his bones with oyster-shells. There's fine oyster-beds in the bay," continued Dodge, carelessly.—"Are you fond of oysters?" The bailiff groaned, but made no audible reply. The scrub grew more dense. "You never fell in with bushrangers, did you?" inquired Dodge.

"No-o," stuttered the bailiff.

"This is a great place for 'em—it is supposed that their head quarters is somewhere in this scrub."

"No-o!! I won't go another step forward," said the now horror-stricken bailiff. "Let us go back." Dodge acquiesced.

One conversant with the ways of the woods would have noticed that at short intervals Dodge, with apparent carelessness, had partially broken off small twigs from the bushes he met with in his progress, as marks to guide him out of the dense scrub into which he had penetrated. His plot was now ripe for execution. Performing some eccentric movements, first proceeding for a short distance in one direction, and suddenly changing it for another, the bailiff was at length completely mystified as to the direction in which he had been travelling.

"Hist! did you hear nothing?" exclaimed Dodge.

"No-o: nothing. What?—Eh?" said the bailiff, and his face was livid with fear.

"There! There!! said Dodge, "don't you see the bushes shaking again?—'tis—the blacks!—the blacks!" he shouted, and in two or three bounds was out of sight.

"Don't leave me!—don't run away! Oh save me!—Save me!" shouted the miserable bailiff; "I shall be roasted and eaten alive—I shall," and he sunk upon the earth.

A savage yell now arose at his very feet.

"O good black fellows—most worthy bushrangers, oh spare me!—spare me!—I'm very old and tough, and shouldn't agree with you. I tell you so as a friend; so don't!—Oh don't!" Hearing a low chuckle close to him, he made several attempts to rise, but he was so entangled in the scrub that he could not do so.

Then there arose such a peal of laughter, so loud and so energetic, that the bailiff buried his face in the earth from very fear. When he lifted it again, the same sounds were ringing in his ears, but at a greater distance.

About an hour afterwards, a man emerged from the scrub dressed in the remains of a flannel shirt and canvass trousers, his face was red, his eyes protruding, and every now and then his cheeks, which at other times were like a shrivelled bladder, would swell out as if on the point of bursting. These alarming symptoms were partially relieved by such hearty laughter

as made the old woods ring again. "Well, well," at length
the individual stammered out, as well as he could from his almost hysterical state, "if *this* example fails, I must clear
out for good." It was old Dodge, who, in a short time reached the creek and paddled himself over, where he found Hugh
and Slinger waiting, with a meal prepared and set forth in true
bush fashion on a large box. "Here I am again," he said; "I
thought my last adventure with bailiffs would have prevented the
necessity for any further cruelty on my part to the species, but
they will not learn wisdom." He then recounted his adventure,
concluding—"a night in the scrubs will cure our friend, I
think, of his partiality for Westernport. It won't be a pay-
ing speculation for him—this won't."

"But," said Slinger, "you surely will not leave the poor
wretch in such a position, and after frightening him as you have
done : why he will die of cold."

"Won't I though," said Dodge. "He will keep warm
until the morning, and by that time have recovered his senses.
Then he will either strike upon the creek or come into open
ground, and the chances are that eventually he will make my
station. Meantime we must clear out."

"Suppose you accompany us in search of a station," said
Slinger; "that is the business we are out upon."

"Agreed," replied Dodge; "and there is no time to be
lost; we must make preparations at once." Accordingly, after
taking out the necessary supplies, he planted his flour-bag and
beef-barrel in the hollow of an adjacent tree, declaring that he
would starve out his enemy in case he attempted to quarter upon him Selecting a pair of not particularly clean canvass
trousers and some strips of linen to serve for strings, he then
observed, "Now I'll show you what I call my *multum in par-
vo ;*" he then proceeded, after tying up the bottom of one

...ers, and bestead; a block of wood answered the double
...ose of chai and pillow, the beef-barrel was also a kind of
...able, whilst the cover of it was made to do duty occasion-
... as a rat-trap by setting it up with a stick and a string, and
...so described the destruction he wrought upon the rat species
...ese simple means as something quite astonishing. After
...ing by no means an uncomfortable evening, a shake-down
...ade and they all turned in.

...fore they ll asleep, a wild dog was heard howling near
...t and presently a chorus struck up. Dodge, taking his
...ent to the door, and answered them by a howl nearly as
...to which tere was a reply. "These chaps and I have a
...onversatic together of a night—they are capital compa-
...nd afford o lots of sport. They smell I've got some
...here again I will be back directly: don't you come,"
..., as the to were preparing to follow him: "it takes an
...nd to toin a wild dog." After he had been gone
...en minute, the report of his gun was heard, and then
...nd barrel In a few minutes he returned dragging a
...og by the eg whilst Lady kept a firm grip of its throat.
...his fellow has made free with my veal, I'll be bound,"
...dge.

...o they ki calves?" Slinger inquired.

...casional, and sheep very often. Why I have scarcely
... on my station with a perfect tail, they generally manage
...off that litle delicacy when it is young, so that I never
...tail soup but I have a capital substitute in that of the
...oo." He then called his dog. "Come here, old girl, I
...o make a olster of you to night," and she lay down in
...enient potion. Old Dodge placed his head on this
...pillow, an was soon snoring lustily, in which he was
joined b his visitors.

of the legs to deposit in it a quantity of flour, that done, he
tied it tightly above; the other leg was devoted to tea, sugar,
and tobacco.   "Let me see," he said, thoughtfully, tapping the
ashes from his pipe, "we have tobacco, flour, tea, sugar, powder, shot, bullets, and blankets; there is only one thing requisite to render us disgustingly rich—a bottle of rum, Slinger,
and we should be rolling in wealth.

"Indeed it would be a comfortable addition," Slinger answered.

Dodge smiled pleasantly as he removed a turf from one
side of his chimney, and thrusting his arm into the aperture
drew forth several black bottles.   One was labelled "lauda-
num—poison," another "the cattle medicine," another "poison for wild dogs."   Selecting the latter, the cork was drawn,
and after drinking to the success of their expedition, Dodge
tendered a portion of the "poison" to his visitors, who partook of the same, found it marvellously like rum to the taste,
and found no ill effects from their libations.   The remainder in
the bottle was then carefully wrapped in a blanket to be taken
with them, and the rest replaced in the chimney.

"There is nothing like preparing for the worst," said Dodge.
—"A man does not like drinking freely from a bottle labelled
'poison,' although the stuff in it may smell like rum.   I wish
education was more general.   Now if the black protectors
had taught the Darkeys to read they would be more careful
how they emptied my poison bottles :—as it is, the rascals some-
how scent 'em out, and not having the fear of death before
their eyes, they get dead drunk on their contents."

Every thing being arranged for an early move on the morrow, the visitors had leisure to admire the domestic arrangements of their host.   The great box, which occupied so conspicuous a position in the hut, served as a table, chest of

drawers, and bedstead; a block of wood answered the double purpose of chair and pillow, the beef-barrel was also a kind of side-table, whilst the cover of it was made to do duty occasionally as a rat-trap by setting it up with a stick and a string, and Dodge described the destruction he wrought upon the rat species by these simple means as something quite astonishing. After spending by no means an uncomfortable evening, a shake-down was made and they all turned in.

Before they fell asleep, a wild dog was heard howling near the hut and presently a chorus struck up. Dodge, taking his gun, went to the door, and answered them by a howl nearly as wild, to which there was a reply. " These chaps and I have a little conversation together of a night—they are capital company, and afford me lots of sport. They smell I've got some grub here again. I will be back directly: don't you come," he said, as the two were preparing to follow him : " it takes an old hand to touch a wild dog." After he had been gone about ten minutes, the report of his gun was heard, and then a second barrel. In a few minutes he returned dragging a large dog by the leg whilst Lady kept a firm grip of its throat.

"This fellow has made free with my veal, I'll be bound," said Dodge.

" Do they kill calves ? " Slinger inquired.

" Occasionally, and sheep very often. Why I have scarcely a beast on my station with a perfect tail, they generally manage to nip off that little delicacy when it is young, so that I never get ox-tail soup ; but I have a capital substitute in that of the kangaroo." He then called his dog. " Come here, old girl, I want to make a bolster of you to night," and she lay down in a convenient position. Old Dodge placed his head on this novel pillow, and was soon snoring lustily, in which he was shortly joined by his visitors.

P

It was fated their slumbers were not to be of long duration, for Lady, the kangaroo dog and pillow, suddenly sprung up with a growl, letting Dodge's head drop heavily upon the ground. The sleepers started up in time to hear a sound as of several persons retreating from the hut. On opening the door, the dog ran out barking furiously, but the inmates could distinguish nothing to excite alarm, although the moon shone brightly.

Dodge was rubbing his head, as he said, "One of the disadvantages of having an animated bolster; but we must look about us; I can't make this out exactly;" and he whistled for his Lady, but she did not return. "Stranger still!" said Dodge. "See to your guns, lads, and follow me, there's no time to dress." Accordingly they wrapped themselves in their blankets and sallied from the hut.

Dodge assumed the command, "Raymond," he said, "you will take the right, I the left, and Slinger, you keep near, don't go above thirty yards off, and if Raymond or I make signals, go inside immediately, and let no one enter but ourselves.—Blaze away, we shan't be far off."

Then they each went on their separate missions. Raymond stumbled over logs and tufts of long grass, for such was his anxiety to discover some cause of alarm that he scarcely looked to see where he was going, and after he had made two or three turns, he began to wonder in which direction the hut was. At this moment he saw an object move out from behind a tree and quickly dart back again. Stealthily advancing to where he had seen the figure, he had reached to within a few yards of the spot, when he heard a low whistle. Raising his gun very cautiously, he dropped among the grass, and shortly afterwards saw a light object protruding from behind the tree. Taking a deliberate aim at it, he said, "Move and I will fire. Who and what are you?"

"Oh only old Dodge," said that personage, coming into full view. "I thought 'twas you. why how did you manage to get my side of the hut? I pushed out my blanket for you to have a shot at. Have you seen anything?"

"No, only your respectable self."

"Well, we must go back again; but it is queer. What can have become of Lady?"

They soon came in sight of Slinger on guard. He had lighted a pipe and was seated upon a log with his back to them.

"Steady," whispered Dodge, "Shall I show you what chance your friend would have with the natives?

"How will you do that?"

"You remain near this tree for five minutes, and you shall see the first lesson the blacks taught me. Now I'm going to make Slinger prisoner before he knows anything about it. Take care of my rifle." He then wriggled himself among the long grass, and was soon lost to Hugh. In a short time he saw Slinger rest his gun against the tree, for the moon was quite clear, and presently Dodge rose close behind him and clasped him tightly in his arms.

"Da——" Slinger began to roar, when Dodge placed his hand upon his mouth.

"It is all right," he said, as he let him go, "don't swear, I told you I would not be far off. Now that is what I call taking advantage of a man behind his back." Hugh ran up, and they all returned to their shake-down, but the dog did not make her appearance.

CHAPTER X.

THE next morning they were astir before that very punctual
and amusing bird, the Laughing Jackass, * had proclaimed to
the sluggards of the bush, by its discordant hootings, that the
sun was again risen upon the land. The note of the More-
pork,† not unlike that of a cuckoo with a cold, the purring
cry of the flying squirrel, and the squall of the several kinds of
opossums, rang in the ears of the little party as they were making final arrangements for their departure. It was at this juncture that the lost dog returned, but in a pitiable plight; she
could scarcely crawl, and her breathing was nearly stopped
from the strangling effects of a strip of linen which tightly en-
circled her throat. Her mouth was covered with foam, and it
appeared as if the poor creature had returned to her master only
to die. Dodge was almost beside himself; and after separating the ligature, and wiping the foam from her mouth, he
fetched some water of which she eagerly partook. Then he addressed her in encouraging accents, interspersed with an occasional malediction upon the heads as well as other portions of
the bodies of her late persecutors. "Poor old girl, keep up
your pluck:" (then some very strong expressions alluding to
eyes and limbs:) "never say 'die.' Havn't we stood by each
other for years? and when the Gorger left me, didn't you stick
to me? to be sure you did. Then cock your tail up—(The
ruffians!—the hang-dog villains!)—Hurra! now you are better—bravo!"

Whether there was something exhilarating in the earnest
manner of Dodge, or that the dog was a proficient in the Eng-

* Called also the Settler's Clock.   † A species of owl

lish language, or more probably, whether the removal of the impediments to her breathing might not have had some effect, the Lady rapidly recovered, and her master's delight was unbounded; and now all anxiety on the score of his dog's life was set at rest, the piece of linen with which she had been tied attracted his attention. He examined the end closely, and gave it as his opinion that some land-lubber, who did not know how to tie a knot, had endeavoured to steal her, but that she had given him the slip by gnawing her fastenings. Unfolding a portion of the linen, he said, "It is a plain stripe and very neat —pretty pattern, isn't it? it is a favourite one with Government, and much in vogue in prisoners' barracks and road-gangs.—Creation!!" he exclaimed, "look here!" There certainly was nothing very tremendous met their gaze, for stamped upon the linen, in unassuming characters, were the letters C. P.

"C. P," said Slinger. "Oh, initial letters of course."

"Yes," said Dodge, "and I'll tell you of what: D—d Villain, Sir." Seeing his listeners were somewhat mystified, he volunteered an explanation,—"C. P. stands for Crown Prisoner, and Crown Prisoner stands for D—d Villain, they are synonymous terms, and it is my firm conviction that our visitors of last night were no better than they should be: however, let us waste no more time, but be off."

With a deep blue sky overhead, and with the dew still upon the sward, they started on their expedition, whilst Lady followed them at a respectful distance. They soon struck on the trail of cattle, and after a little observation, Dodge was satisfied it was of his own herd, and that they had taken the direction of the mountain ranges and were completely out of harm's way.

After skirting the creek, (the water of which was brackish) for several miles, they stopped for mid-day rest and refreshment

under the shade of a fern tree. The explorers found themselves
at the base of a range of hills covered with timber, which were
succeeded by yet higher ranges, until in the extreme distance
the craggy peaks of mountains were seen capped with snow.
Hitherto they had passed over low undulating thinly timbered
land, and the contrast afforded by the prospect before them was
very great. To penetrate the unknown region bid fair to tax
all their energies as well as patience, but there was the attrac-
tion of novelty; so that when they deliberated upon which
course to take, it was unanimously determined that an endeavour should be made to penetrate through the scrub, which
stood like a barrier betwixt them and the distant hills.

" In all cases of difficulty," said Dodge, "there's nothing
like a pipe of tobacco : it affords a man opportunity for thought.
Now I am in doubt where we had best strike into the scrub,
so we will smoke over it." He was soon enveloped in fragrant
clouds from his pipe, which was quite an antiquity. " Really,"
he said, between the puffs, "the way some smoke in this country is dreadful—moderation in all things, I say. I take one
pipe the first thing in the morning to destroy the effects of the
night dews, one or two after breakfast to fit me for my day's
work, two or three after dinner to promote digestion, and a few
after I have turned in at night to keep off mosquitoes. A man
can scarcely be more moderate than that, I think." Whatever
his friends might have thought, they did not feel disposed to
dispute the proposition.

After Dodge had been silent for a short time, he exclaimed,
"We must go through it;" and depositing the pipe in his
pouch, he flourished his tomahawk, and, joined by Hugh and
Slinger, they commenced a vigorous attack upon the part of the
scrub which seemed most likely to give way under their exertions. After working for several hours most energetically they

found there was no indication of the scrub getting more prac-
ticable, but rather the reverse. Dodge was too true a bushman to allow himself to be beaten by any ordinary impediments, but his experience satisfied him that they had made their
attempt at an unfortunate point. In this dilemma he again had
recourse to his pipe. "There is nothing for it I'm afraid," he
said, "but to turn back. I like going ahead, but we must
knock under for the present. We will camp upon the plains
to night, and try what is to be done to-morrow." They soon
retraced the ground they had experienced so much difficulty in
gaining, and once more found themselves, not much improved
in appearance, in open country. Here Dodge set to work with
scarcely less energy than he had hitherto displayed, to erect a
shelter for the night, as there were indications of rain. Setting
two stout forked sticks in the ground about ten feet apart, he
rested a long pole upon them, thus forming a kind of roof-tree;
then he stripped some sheets of bark, about eight feet in length
and from two to three feet broad, and rested them in a horizontal
position against the pole, lapping the edge of each sheet over
the other; a pile of branches from the neighbouring trees were
placed at either end of this primitive structure; a large heap
of dried wood was collected; and then Dodge expressed a fervent wish that all the world was as well off as themselves: "but
there is one drawback," he said, "to this delightful building
site :—where can we get fresh water?" It was true, they had
sufficient to serve for the evening, but from whence were they
to draw their supply for the ensuing day? Dodge was prepared: *he* knew, after looking into the sky, now quite overcast,
and listening to the low sighing of the wind through the fibre-
like foliage of the she-oak trees.

In the course of the day Lady had killed a bandicoot, of
which Dodge possessed himself, and whilst the adventurers were

enjoying their tea and damper, the dog was by no means badly provided with food.

Soon after nightfall, the fatigues they had undergone began to tell upon the wanderers. Without divesting themselves of their clothes, they were but too glad to make such other preparations for comfortably reposing as circumstances permitted. In consideration of the hard usage Lady had recently undergone, she was permitted to rest under the same shelter as her master, and it was not long before all were wrapped in profound sleep.

After the lapse of some hours, one of a party of five men approached the sleepers noiselessly : he was heavily armed. By the light of the fire he examined their forms, and was retiring, apparently satisfied with his scrutiny, when his attention appeared to be suddenly arrested ; a slight breeze had blown up a momentary flame, but it was sufficiently lasting to illuminate Raymond's features, and to strike something like terror into the heart of his contemplator. Scarcely daring to look again, he fell back and joined his companions, who remained at a short distance.

These men were a part of Bayley's (the bushranger's) gang, who, finding the Sydney side was scoured by the troops and police, had unconsciously followed the same route as their late leader, with the view of seizing a boat or vessel in Westernport and escaping. Their object was to procure a good supply of provisions, and to sail to one of the numerous islands in Bass's Straits.

" Why you look as if you'd seen the devil," said one.

" And supposing I were to tell you I had : what then ? "

" The only remark I should have to offer," said the first speaker, " would be, that we are giving ourselves unnecessary trouble. he generally looks after us, not we after him. But can you see any stores there ? if there are, we must have them if it cost us a fight—devil or no devil, it's all one to hungry men."

"No: I saw no stores," said the man who, for the present, we shall call the Scout: "but I saw a face there, which by some strange fascination, reminded me of a gallows."

"Some of our own kidney?" inquired the other.

"No: not so. The gallows I thought of was for myself."

"You white-livered coward," said the first, "you are fit for nothing but the gallows: it will be only a natural death for you. Tell me what makes your flesh tremble on your bones and the muscles of that ugly parchment face of yours twitch as if the rope was already round your neck."

"Don't talk so loud nor so disagreeably," said the Scout, "one sleeps not far off who would hang us all."

This information was not received without surprise.

"He can," repeated the Scout, "if we leave him the chance. His father helped to transport me   I should like to see him shot, and should not mind doing it myself just to get my hand in," and his voice trembled as he spoke.

"Bravo! old parchment face," said the one who had taunted him with cowardice: "shoot him from behind, lest his gallows face should spoil your aim."

After the conversation already narrated, they fell back some distance from the sleepers, but the Scout returned by himself.

Dodge was at all times a light sleeper, and it happened that he had turned out to make up the fire, when he detected the sound of human voices floating down upon the night air. With a mind more alive to bailiffs than bushrangers, he left the fire untouched and crawled to a tree a few yards away from his sleeping-place, where the glare of the embers did not interfere with his scrutiny of surrounding objects. He had not long

Q

held his position before he detected the figure of a man emerging from the darkness, apparently making for the same tree; in a short time he reached it, and looking intently upon the sleepers, he partly raised his weapon, but seemed unable to proceed further in his purpose; at length Dodge saw the muzzle of the piece taking a line in the direction of Raymond's head. As quick as thought, with one hand he struck the weapon up, and with the other seized its bearer by the throat, dragging him towards the little light afforded by the embers. The scuffling awoke the sleepers, who started on their legs in time to see the Scout kicked off his, and Dodge, still holding him by the throat, threw himself with all his weight upon the body of his nearly exhausted antagonist. "Aha! my chicken," he said, after gathering breath a little, "is shooting gentlemen a favourite sport of your's?" But the scout's powers of utterance were confined to a low moaning, although the grasp upon his throat was loosened. "Make a blaze," said Dodge, "light some dried leaves; bear a hand, and strip up a blanket; we will secure our friend here while he is quiet." Before his instructions could be carried into effect, the Scout partially recovered and evinced a disposition to regain his liberty.

"Listen to me," said Dodge, grasping his gun, "there ain't two ways about me; I say, and I do. You are my prisoner, made so just in time to save you from murdering my friend. Now," he said, cocking his piece, "you hear that—the snap's up: attempt to get upon your legs, and the snap will be down, and so you will be, for I'll shoot you with as little compunction as I would a wild dog."

It was some time before the prisoner was effectually secured: this was done by wrapping him tightly in strips of blanket; during the performance of which operation Dodge consoled him by telling him he would surely be hanged.—"You will swing," said he, "as sure as a gun—in fact, much surer than that old iron tube of your's."

"Just light some leaves, lads, and let us see this fellow's face."

A blaze was soon made, and the surprise of Raymond was extreme when it lighted up the horror-stricken features of the felon-lawyer Jarrol.

He was in the midst of explaining to his companions the reason of his confusion, when they were all rendered speechless by hearing a voice close by them exclaim "On your lives don't move a limb."

All eyes were bent upon the figure of a tall man who stood before them, his gun levelled and within a few feet of their heads. Hugh and Slinger had no difficulty in recognising the form and features of Bayley. Stooping down, yet still prepared for imme-diate action, he raised the prostrate Jarrol and lifting him upon one of his shoulders, he stalked away into the darkness, with his face still bent upon the wonder-stricken travellers. It was not before his form was nearly lost in the gloom that Dodge seized a gun and was preparing to follow, but he was restrained by Slinger.—"That fellow deserves all his luck," he said, "bushranger or whatever he is, who ventured so much to save a comrade."

"I should like to have picked off the lawyer for all that," said Dodge.

It becomes necessary for us to explain the causes which bring Bayley again before our readers.

When the bailiff succeeded in escaping from the scrub, which he did at an angle of the creek contiguous to Bayley's tree, it is not surprising that the watchful eye of the bush-ranger, who still found it convenient to occupy his old stronghold, soon discovered that the subject of his observation was in a state of bewilderment, and utterly lost as to the direction he should follow. As he advanced towards him, the bailiff was only too glad to recognise the form of a human being. After he had partaken of some food, and recounted his adventures with the imaginary bushrangers, Bayley put him in the right direction for Melbourne and left him.

Thinking the bushrangers the bailiff had spoken of might be a portion of his own gang, and finding how utterly hopeless his chances of escape alone were, he determined, in preference to the miserable life he had lately led, to endeavour to find them, and then to concert together a plan of operations. After walking some miles, he discovered the trail of five men, and following it up vigorously, he found himself ere long in the neighbourhood, not only of the bushrangers, but also of a party of white men.

It was whilst in ambush near that he discovered the latter had made a prisoner of one of the gang, and he determined to attempt a rescue, conceiving that whoever he might be, he should bind him in such ties of gratitude, that he would be a wretch indeed to prove unfaithful. We have seen with what daring his design was executed.

It was not until Jarrol had been borne some distance, and was released from his bonds, that the rescuer and the rescued recognised each other, and when they did, it afforded Bayley but little satisfaction. "I have saved you from swinging," he said, "I ask only good faith in return."

Jarrol had commenced a speech full of protestations of gratitude, but he was stopped by Bayley.

"I want it in actions not in words, we may be of service to each other."

As soon as Jarrol explained the views he and his companions entertained in coming to Westernport, Bayley's original design was confirmed; he would escape with them.

"Have they heard anything of a reward for my apprehension, and yours, or any of the gang?"

"We heard something of the kind, but what is offered?"

"Two hundred pounds and a free pardon to any man turning traitor. Do you think there are any in the band who would sell me or others so cheaply?"

"I think we are quite safe so far as that goes."

"Then if the object of my men is only to escape, I will lead them again, but if to plunder, no."

"You are conscientious," said Jarrol, "I hope to have your assistance yet in transacting a little business before we leave this part of the country."

"What may it be?" said Bayley.

"A mere trifle, I have a score to settle with one of those fellows from whom you rescued me."

"I will not injure him, and you shall not," said Bayley with energy, "let me hear no more about it if you value my good will."

"I *shall* not, who will prevent me?"

"I will."

"Indeed!".

"Yes, Jarrol," Bayley said in an impressive tone, "I will never permit it, and in cold blood too! Have you so soon forgotten your escape from the gallows?"

"Well, Captain Bayley," said Jarrol, "you have earned my gratitude, and you shall have it."

CHAPTER XI.

WE need scarcely say, that after the adventure we have narrated, sleep forsook the little party with whom we have more particularly to deal. The sudden appearance and disappearance of Jarrol seemed almost like a dream, and the explorers would willingly have resigned the object which had brought them into the part of the country where they found themselves, had their more experienced companion held out the least hope of a successful pursuit; but the rain which had threatened on the previous evening now poured down in torrents, so as effectually to obliterate every track which the disturbers of their last night's slumbers were likely to leave behind them, they therefore determined, as soon as the weather cleared, on prosecuting the search for a station amongst the hills.

"Now, my boys!" said Dodge, "we must collect some tea-water while the rain lasts, and I'll show you how to set to work." Taking out a moderately clean towel and a tin pot from his budget, he walked amongst the wet grass trailing the towel after him, and when it was sufficiently saturated for his purpose he wrung it carefully into the pot; after many repetitions of the same process he returned to the fire with about a pint of very doubtful looking water. "You see," he said, " I would willingly share it with you; but may be, as you are young bushmen, you would find it more agreeable to use your own towels."

Neither Hugh nor Slinger were yet sufficiently thirsty to have recourse to the plan they had seen practised, but they collected some water by catching it as it trickled from the pieces of bark which served them as a shelter from the weather. Dodge suggested that as they would find the water they had procured was not drinkable, they might indulge in a wash, and then follow his example, or they would have to start without a breakfast. Even the dog Lady refused the water. Both in appearance and smell it strongly resembled the liquid usually found in tan-pits; in truth, from the manner in which it was procured there is little doubt that it bore a nearer similitude than simply in appearance.

"Now really," said Dodge, as Slinger was making a desperate effort to taste it, "you had better not: I usually take such stuff as that for physic, of which I have only two sorts; one is the juice from the bark of the gum tree, and the other sea water, half-a-pint to a dose. But you may rely upon it, the best stuff to make tea of, when you are hard up, is rain water filtered through a snow-white towel. Now try it, do: there's nothing like it. Come, taste mine, it's capital." But our friends were not quite bushmen enough for that. "Well," said Dodge, "I shall bottle some, and advise you to do the same, in case we should not fall in with a stream to day."

As animal food formed no part of their stores, and the rain ceasing, it was considered advisable to try the neighbourhood for a kangaroo or wallaby before finally bidding adieu to the plains. The intelligent Lady appeared to be quite aware of the necessity of providing for the future, and she was most obedient to her master's commands. Very suddenly Dodge came to a halt, and calling her to his side, desired his friends to look at the picture before them. It was some minutes before they espied several kangaroos feeding quietly in an open space about two hundred yards distant. Giving directions to his friends to conceal themselves in the grass, Dodge retreated, still watching every movement of the animals, until he reached a neighbouring tree. Plucking some small branches which he arranged so as to form a screen, easily carried before him with one hand, he advanced upon his prey, in a direction favourable for the accomplishment of his purpose, and had nearly reached within gunshot, when a slight shifting of the breeze warned the sensitive animals of approaching danger : they ceased to feed, and appeared uneasy and watchful.* These signs were not lost upon the wary old bushman, who remained stationary for some minutes, when a further variation of the wind came kindly to his aid, and he again advanced. As soon as he had reached within gun-shot, he dropped the screen of leaves, and the next moment the report of his gun was heard echoing amongst the neighbouring hills.   The result of the shot was soon manifest, for a large old man kangaroo, badly wounded, was seen struggling with Dodge and his dog; the latter had fixed her teeth in her adversary's neck, whilst her master had seized its tail, and both were being dragged and jerked about in a most unceremonious manner, without much opportunity of making any resistance.   The two friends reaching the scene of action, soon changed the aspect of affairs, and increased the prospect of a substantial meal.   The kangaroo, confused amongst its numerous foes, before long afforded an opportunity which Dodge quickly embraced.   Drawing his knife, with one sweep of his arm he separated the ham-strings of his antagonist, and laid him powerless at his feet; once there, he was soon dispatched, and a quarter of an hour sufficed for cutting him up, and each man bore off a share of the booty.

"I *could* tell you a story, and a true one too," said Dodge, "only I'm afraid you are tired of hearing me talk so much about myself, tho' for the matter of that, what else can a man be expected to talk about when he has had very little company but himself for half his life."   As Dodge found his companions willing to listen, he commenced his story.

* The sense of smell in the kangaroo is most acute.

"When I made my first excursion into the bush, my mind was well crammed with dreadful yarns of bush-rangers and blacks. I left the town armed for a fight, and the weight of the ammunition I carried far exceeded that of my grub. I have grown wiser since then. The object I had in view was to find out an old friend and schoolfellow who had located on the Goulburn. You will not be surprised to hear that more than once on my journey I got out of my reckoning, and one evening, after a day's wandering, scarcely knowing in what direction, it was with no slight degree of satisfaction I saw a hut in the distance. On reaching it I found it occupied by two men, whose appearance made me almost regret I had fallen in with them. One was deformed, his face was nearly hidden by a crop of red whiskers, that part of it which was to be seen was not calculated to make a favorable impression upon a stranger. His 'chum,' as he called him, was quite as ill-looking, with the additional disadvantage that all his face was exposed, for he had no whiskers. They gave me a surly welcome, and a feed off a kangaroo haunch, and I thought they appeared anxious that I should turn in, which I was not sorry to do, being very tired. A loud peal of thunder awakened me out of a dream in which, I remember, two ruffianly bushrangers, the counterparts of my entertainers, played a horribly conspicuous part. As I awoke I saw the two men seated over the fire, and my dream seemed to have assumed a reality : they were whispering and muttering indistinctly to each other. Hearing the words 'old man' repeated frequently, I listened more attentively. 'He died game though,' said one, 'the first shot smashed his arm, but he fought well arder that. I settled him at last, though'—and here he drew his hand across his throat. I felt anything but comfortable, and my suspicions were not relieved by the events which ensued.

R

" 'Where did you stow him?' inquired the deformed one.

" 'Outside,' was the reply; 'and now I think on it, I should have put him out of sight: I'll do it at once.' He left the hut for a few moments, and returned with his hands smeared with blood.

"I need not tell you I slept no more for that night, and that I left as early as I could the next morning without exciting suspicion. Not far from the hut I passed a heap of bark, a little pool of blood stood near it which had trickled from some object—I had little doubt what that object was—hidden underneath.

"Very soon after leaving, I was fortunate in meeting with the settler to whom the hut belonged, in which I had slept, and I told him of the conversation I had overheard, and my impression that some dark deed had been committed. We returned together, and I could see that my sudden re-appearance took the inmates quite by surprise. The master asked a few common-place questions, to which it struck me the answers were unsatisfactory and confused.

"Without further hesitation I led him to the heap of bark, underneath which, I had little doubt, lay the victim of a barbarous deed. As the horrible mystery was being revealed, I was not surprised to find the two men narrowly observing our motions from the hut, but when the removal of the last sheet of bark was accompanied by a loud roar of laughter from the owner of the station, I *was* considerably flabbergasted.—'Oh murder! murder!!" he cried, 'I shall die o'laughing—why it's an old man sure enough.' There indeed lay the body, but it was of *an old man kangaroo*—a regular boomer: there was a gash across the throat and one fore arm was broken. Didn't I feel uncommonly small at the 'dreadful revelation.' So the murder was out. Now for the moral," said Dodge, assuming a look of mock gravity.—"Don't put down the ugliest fellows for the greatest rascals, nor jump at conclusions on hearing only the fag end of a yarn."

After our explorers had spent several days and had penetrated some distance into the ranges at the back of Westernport, they could well have imagined themselves in another land. The country was altogether of a different character to any which they had yet passed through. They travelled in the midst of gloom, for the foliage of the lofty trees meeting far overhead, prevented more than an occasional stream of sun-light falling upon the moist earth. The air was laden with a scent of musk which became most oppressive, though the silvery leaves of the straggling shrubs from whence the odour proceeded tended slightly to enliven the prospect. Though the sun had risen some hours, yet the atmosphere was humid and unwholesome. The general silence which prevailed became painfully perceptible by the distinctness with which each drop of water could be heard as it fell on the underlaying leaves, seemingly accompanied by tiny echoes. During the day few sounds of birds or beasts, nor even of insects, helped to dispel the universal gloom. The valleys were, if possible, more thickly timbered than the tops of the hills. They abounded with tree ferns, which there appeared to attain their greatest luxuriance. Such was the general character of the region through which they were passing.

"This don't suit me," said Dodge, almost out of temper; "I don't want to learn the philosophy of a man's eating his boots: I'm not so fond of leather as that; and I don't wish to enjoy such an appetite as would induce me to eat a black fellow stuffed with broken bottles, and I like to know when it's day and when it's night—this ain't neither, and I don't like your high districts: I like a low neighbourhood. A pretty place this in which to be hard up for grub—I haven't seen so much as a fly-ing squirrel for the last two days."

"Never say die," said Slinger encouragingly.

"Of course not," said Dodge, "I ain't saying die, am I? Excuse me, if I'm hasty; but there's two things I must have, my baccy and my grub, and I'm nearly out of both; so are you: my opinion is, we shall find nothing good in this quarter, and that the sooner we leave it the better." So it was at once agreed they should retrace their steps, and Dodge thereupon recovered his wonted good humour. Nothing seemed to escape his notice, and every hollow tree engaged his especial attention.

Whether it was that the effects of hunger lent an additional keenness to his faculties, we will not take upon us to say, but discovering the track of some animal upon the ground he fol-lowed it carefully, and finding it terminated at the base of a towering gum tree, upon the bark of which some scratches were visible, he was induced to look higher, and soon espied, perched on one of the topmost branches, an animal, which at the great height, looked scarcely larger than a rat. As he was seeking the most favorable spot from whence to bring down his game, he issued the following verbal invitation, "Mr. Dodge hopes shortly to have the pleasure of Messrs. Slinger and Raymond's company to dinner, and begs to intimate the convenience they will expe-rience in bringing their own knives, forks, and plates. No an-swer required." As he uttered the last words, the crack of his rifle was heard, and before its echo had ceased, the luckless *carbora** fell crashing through the branches and lay dead upon the ground. A quarter of an hour found it cooking before a fire large enough to have roasted a sheep instead of an animal not half the size. When served up (which it was on a piece of dried bark) they

---

* The native name of an animal of the sloth species, but incorrectly called by the colonists, a bear

found it anything but palatable, for it proved to be little more than bone and sinew. After making a series of attacks upon one leg but with small results, Dodge at last resigned it in despair to Lady, and selecting a more promising portion, laid it on a fallen tree, and substituting his tomahawk for his teeth, chopped it vigorously for some time, and at length succeeded in reducing it to such a state that he was enabled to satisfy the cravings of hunger.

They experienced no difficulty in retracing their steps for the first day or two after turning their faces towards home, the tracks then grew more and more indistinct, until at last Dodge advised pushing on in a direction which he indicated, and which in his opinion, bid fair to lead them out of the scrubs. The latter inducement lent energy to their exertions, and with stout hearts, though with empty provision-bags, they commenced their arduous task, now rendered doubly hazardous by a sense of weakness, the result of privations already undergone.

It was after a more than usually fatiguing day, and whilst preparing to camp, that Dodge was startled by discovering tracks indicating that some blacks had recently been in the locality. His olfactory powers were also put to the test, and he positively asserted that he could smell fire not far distant. After ruminating on this new and unexpected difficulty, Dodge expressed great apprehension that the blacks, who he was quite satisfied were in the neighbourhood, belonged to one of the untamed Gipps land tribes who occasionally made a foray across the mountains separating their country from Westernport. He would allow no tomahawk to be used nor any unnecessary noise made in constructing a shelter for the night; he was also very scrupulous respecting the fire, which he would not allow to be lighted before a pit had been dug sufficiently deep to prevent the flames rising above the level of the ground. As soon as

darkness set in, Dodge desired his friends to resign themselves
to sleep, which he assured them they might do with safety, as
very few of the native tribes ventured to move abroad after dark.
For himself he had decided upon reconnoitering in the neighbourhood, and under the cloak of night to discover where the
blacks had pitched their camp, and to make such observations
as might serve him on the morrow.   Arming himself with care,
he left Raymond and Slinger in no very amiable state of mind
on account of his positive refusal to allow them to accompany
him, notwithstanding they made great efforts to shake his resolution.   He stalked away noiselessly, after giving his friends
warning not to mistake him for a black when he returned.   The
two friends watched for a time, but sleep at length overcame
their resolution to remain awake until the return of their absent
companion.

In the course of a short time, with legs bruised and bleeding, Dodge found himself suddenly immersed in a stream into
which he had stumbled.   If something like a subdued curse
escaped him, let us consider for a moment the unenviable position which he occupied.   The night was dark, he was up to his
waist in water, in an unknown district with two friends entirely
dependent upon his guidance, an empty commissariat, and with
every appearance of a new difficulty in the shape of a tribe of
hostile savages.   It is not to be wondered at that his usual
equanimity and coolness momentarily forsook him.   The stream
into which Dodge had fallen was almost overgrown with trees,
and it was some moments before he could extricate himself
from his uncomfortable situation.   As soon as he was fairly on
terra firma his gun and ammunition engaged all his attention.
He was glad to find, as far as he was enabled to discover, that
the wet had not affected either.   After giving himself a shake
or two, he carefully followed the winding of the stream, and

had not gone far before he detected a glimmering light in the
direction he was going. With increased caution he went on
his way, and conjecturing, from the fact of several more fires
becoming visible, that he had come upon the camp of natives,
he got into the bed of the stream in order to avoid leaving any
tracks behind him : in this way he soon came abreast of the en-
campment. There were about thirty *weelems,* or rude huts,
pitched upon the side of a hill, at the base of which the stream
ran. The night was cold, and it would have afforded Dodge
infinite satisfaction to have left his watery bed and warmed his
benumbed limbs at one of the largest of the fires, around which
several warriors were conversing in a dialect quite unknown to
the watcher. In consequence of the danger which would have
attended the use of his pipe, poor Dodge was fain to dispose of
a portion of the small store of tobacco he had remaining in another way—alas! for the result. The juice of the weed affected
him with a severe fit of coughing which all his efforts were unable to repress, and in a moment the whole camp was in an
uproar. A shower of fire-sticks were cast in the direction from
whence the sound had proceeded, but they revealed nothing.
Dodge foreseeing the turn matters were likely to take had crept
into a clump of tall reeds which were at hand : his position was
one of extreme danger, but that only rendered his brain more
prolific in expedients. Being well aware of the extreme timi-
dity and superstition of the natives at any disturbance by night,
and also that there was a universal belief amongst all the tribes
that darkness was the favorite time when *Bund-gil-carno,* the
evil spirit, chiefly delighted to take his walks abroad, his plans
were soon matured—he would play the very deuce. He pluck-
ed a broad leaf from the stem of a reed, and by holding it in a
peculiar manner between his hands and blowing upon it strongly, he produced such a series of unearthly sounds as might well,

in the dead of night, have startled men of greater courage than
Australian blacks.   These noises, interspersed with horrible
shrieks and yells, produced a general panic.   First the women
and children, then the old men and warriors, fled in a body,
leaving Dodge master of the situation.   His first act, after
emerging from his concealment, was to collect the spears, clubs,
and other weapons, which lay scattered about the huts, and to
heap them on one of the fires, at which he was composedly
warming himself, when his dog Lady crept up and laid herself
at his feet.

   " What business have you here, old girl, eh ? " said Dodge,
patting her head, " are you come to take me the nearest way
back ?   Well, I'm ready to start, so ' show home.' "   But Lady
evinced no such disposition ; she went foraging about amongst
the huts, and presently returned to Dodge with a lump of kangaroo's flesh in her mouth.

   " Well thought of, old girl," said Dodge ; " of course we
must sack the town now it is taken, so let us set to work."   In
a very short time he found himself laden with a large stock of
provisions, and, escorted by Lady, who led the way, he was not
long in reaching the locality of his friends.

   They had been awakened by the shouting, and would have
started in search of Dodge had he not previously to leaving them
interdicted such a course under any circumstances.   They had
however, prepared their arms and were so satisfied that *something*
was necessary to be done, that no sooner did Dodge appear than,
without any warning, Slinger let fly at him, fortunately without
fatal effect.

   " That's a good shot," said Dodge, coming forward to the
fire with the utmost coolness, and displaying to the penitent
Slinger a hole made by the bullet in the side of his hat.—"That's
a good shot, but the safest plan always is not to be hasty, and

not to aim too high. Now if that shot of your's, had been made rather lower, you would have been in a pretty fix, and I should have been out of it."

After recounting all that had befallen him since leaving, Dodge concluded by desiring them, as soon as they had refreshed, to prepare for starting. "Eat plenty of the kangaroo," he said, as he laid several large lumps of the flesh before them, "but be very sparing of the flour." The latter warning was not altogether unnecessary, for their stock of "the staff of life" was grown very slender. A very little flour, just sufficient to make, when mixed with water, about half a pint of rather thin paste, was all either of our friends could afford to expend at a single meal.

Concluding from the quantity of flesh found at the camp that the late occupiers must recently have come from the plains, and that the fright they had experienced in the night would probably induce them to return thither, Dodge determined to adopt the hazardous expedient of following their trail. The party set off in Indian file, Dodge taking the lead. They soon reached a more level and open country. During the afternoon a deep, though not wide, river barred their progress. Choosing a convenient situation to occupy for the night, advantage was taken of the daylight to look about them. Several gum trees were observed to have been denuded of very large sheets of bark, which Dodge was not long in declaring had been done for the purpose of constructing canoes, and that in all probability one might be found by making a careful search along the banks of the river on the opposite shore. For Dodge to strip and plunge in was only the work of a minute, in another he was across and lost amongst the tall reeds which lined the stream. Presently a long sheet of bark, which scarcely floated, was thrust forcibly towards our friends, and Dodge followed and prevented it from sinking.

s

"I can't say much for the safety or appearance of the craft at present," he said, scrambling out, "but we must tinker her up to serve our turn. We will cruise down the stream tomorrow. We are not far from the plains. See how sluggishly the river runs." The canoe (it scarcely deserved the name,) was drawn out, and after a minute examination, Dodge considered she might be made available by plastering up her two ends with mud and filling several rather serious-looking fractures with the same humble material. When all the repairs possible had been done, and she really kept free of water, Slinger proposed three cheers for their success.

"Steady," said Dodge, clapping his hand before Slinger's mouth, "there's time enough for that when we are out of hearing of the natives; at present I am not quite sure that we are. Make a better use of your time, and sleep two hours in one. My word! we shall not reach home for a few days if all turns out right, and we must be moving sufficiently early tomorrow to get some two miles down the river ere the sun rises."

Long before daybreak Dodge roused his friends, who were most unwilling to respond to the call. So he set to work and boiled some small portions of tea and sugar, which he succeeded in bringing to light from the inmost recesses of the leg of the pair of trousers in which it will be remembered he ingeniously contrived to stow away all his stores. "This kind of beverage requires to be taken hot," Dodge said, as he, accidentally of course, spilt a little upon Slinger's blanket under which he yet remained coiled; "by drinking it then you will not know whether it is double distilled or not. Come, be alive!" he went on to say, shaking his friends and almost lifting them upon their legs; "be alive, my boat is on the shore, and my bark is — where?" he said, casting his eyes in the direction in which he had left the canoe over-night; his bark was not there.

Further observation confirmed his belief that the river was a tidal one, and that the plains and the bay of Westernport were not far off. They were not long in recovering the canoe, which was found entangled in the boughs of a tree which overhung the water not far from the spot where they had slept. To get in her with their baggage was a very ticklish affair indeed, and even when once afloat extreme caution was requisite to prevent an upset. Dodge had provided himself with a short pole by means of which he paddled down the stream, and by great dexterity and some experience he avoided many impediments which beset his progress.

As the first blush of morning was tinting the hills, now some distance in the rear, and as our friends were congratulating themselves on the success which had hitherto attended their voyaging, a disagreeable grating was felt under the frail vessel and the splintered end of the bough of a tree made its appearance through the bottom of the canoe. "Sit still," said Dodge, "be steady, and she won't capsize: you shan't drown if she does. Sit more my end, Slinger; Raymond, handle some of the spare mud, and as soon as she clears the snag, which she will do as soon as I am overboard, caulk her—dab up the hole." As Dodge spoke the last words he stepped lightly to a partially immersed limb of the tree of which the offending bough also formed a portion, and gradually relieved the canoe of his weight though at the expense of a ducking. As she rose the hole was stopped with mud, but there appeared a prospect of her momentarily parting amidships, so she was hastily dragged ashore and overhauled, when the damages were found to be of such a nature that she was forthwith abandoned.

A rising ground near attracted their attention, and on gaining the summit, a part of the bay of Westernport was plainly seen, whilst the undulating country which intervened was clothed with the richest verdure. Dodge recognised some distant hills as being in the neighbourhood of his station, now some twenty miles distant. "If we had looked nearer home at first," said Dodge, "we should have done as well, and not have been half starved as we are; however, here is something like a cattle run for you, with miles of water frontage, and room to pasture half the stock in the country. We will just take the bearings of it carefully, for I once knew a man who spent two months in looking for a station, and having found one suitable he returned for his cattle, and never could hit upon it afterwards." This was an event not very likely to occur in the present instance, the landmarks were so well defined, and after a few necessary observations, the party set off in high glee at the prospect of soon again reaching Dodge's station, or, as he would insist on calling it "home." We will leave them to pursue their way, whilst we return for a time to the bushrangers, Bayley and Jarrol.

CHAPTER XII.

WHEN Jarrol became aware of the actual terms offered for Bayley's apprehension, and after the latter had made his views known to him, Jarrol became for a time taciturn and thoughtful. Then he suggested to Bayley whether it would not be well to cease all connection with the gang, and for them to try and get off alone. Bayley was soon induced to adopt this view, and his hearty and unsuspecting acquiescence seemed to afford Jarrol intense satisfaction.

It was on the evening before the return of the exploring

party that the two bushrangers took possession of Dodge's apparently deserted hut, intending to occupy it so long as circumstances might render convenient. A quantity of leaves were strewed upon the ground over which some dried grass had been scattered. On this rough pallet the outlaws stretched their weary limbs, and seemed desirous of resigning themselves to slumber. Although both remained silent for some time neither slept, and an observer would have detected certain suspicious glances which Jarrol cast now and then towards the clouded countenance of his companion. If he fancied he could detect the workings of the mind beneath, his conclusions were very far from the truth. Bayley had been looking earnestly into the fire for some moments half unconscious of the presence of another, when he rose, and after pacing up and down the hut once or twice he said abruptly, "Did you ever pray, Jarrol?"

"Why what makes you ask such a question now?" said Jarrol, "'tis not for us to talk of prayer. Come, sit down and tell me some of your adventures." But Bayley again seated himself, and silently buried his face in the folds of his blanket. Jarrol availed himself of the opportunity to remove the caps from Bayley's gun, and placed others in their stead from which he had previously extracted the detonating substance, thus rendering the weapon useless. Bayley soon laid himself out with a deep sigh and fell asleep. Jarrol played the hypocrite for awhile, he then noiselessly arose and taking a heavy brand from the fire he struck his late deliverer a cruel blow upon the temple. The wounded man rolled over with a deep groan and grasped his gun, but the blow was repeated and again a third time, until the victim lay stunned and helpless. Jarrol scarcely dared to look upon the quivering body, but it was necessary for his own safety and the furtherance of his designs that Bayley should be secured whilst in his present state. Accordingly he proceeded to lash his prisoner's arms tightly behind him with a cotton neckerchief, and to do so effectually he applied a stick in the manner of a tourniquet, using such strength that the handkerchief was deeply buried in the flesh. He then swathed the lower parts of the body of his prostrate victim in a blanket, fastening it so securely as to leave scarcely the least power of motion.

It was some time before Bayley evinced any signs of consciousness; when he did it was by groaning and entreating that his arms might be set free. Meeting with no response, he glanced round the hut, and the color returned to his face as he exclaimed in broken accents, "So they've got me at last: well, I know the worst now.—What! have they the both of us?" he said, as his eye rested on Jarrol, who set rocking himself to and fro upon the ground.

Steeped to the lips in crime as he was, and meditating a greater one than any he had ever committed, Jarrol could not look his questioner in the face as he replied, "The police are not here yet, I am going to fetch them."

"This is a rough joke," said Bayley; "come, come, it is time 'twas over; unloose me, let me go, I am in great pain; come, I know 'tis a joke."

"I'm glad you think so; if swinging is a joke, this is one. To be plain with you, you are a prisoner. I mean to sell you for £200 and my free pardon."

Bayley was stupified for a time, at last he said, "So you can sell the man who saved you?"

"Saved me! what was the use of saving me to remain a bushranger? I must save myself now in reality and be a free man again."

"Ungrateful wretch," said Bayley, "I will not ask my life of you:" as he finished speaking every muscle of his frame

seemed to be writhing in agony, his face assumed an expres
sion of fearful rage, and the veins in his forehead swelled almost
to bursting, after a time his countenance assumed more its
usual expression, and he appeared to have fainted.

Jarrol looked on this scene holding his gun in readiness for
action, fearing Bayley might free himself. On seeing his contortions subside, and fearing he might die, he loosened a band
which was round his chest.

"Water, water," Bayley moaned; "quick, quick, or I shall
die; the water is about a hundred yards to the back of the
hut;" this was said in a firmer voice. Jarrol resting his gun
against the wall ran off in the direction indicated.

He was no sooner gone than the prisoner rolled himself into the embers of the fire. Not a groan, not even a sigh, escaped him as his bonds were burning and his flesh scorching.
The bandages about his legs burst one after the other, but his
arms were still bound, when he heard the sound of returning
footsteps. By a desperate effort, but in acute agony, he wrenched the neckerchief into pieces. His limbs were unbound, but
he stood a pitiable object. He tottered to the door picking up
Jarrol's gun on his way thither. There he waited for the return of his would-be betrayer, who rushed into the hut, and the
moment he entered, the door was closed. Bayley stood free
before him. Both regarded each other in silence for several
minutes. "'Tis well for you if you are spending the little time
you have to live in prayer," said Bayley, in a quiet voice.

"No! no! don't say that Captain Bayley, I always liked
you. I—I—will give you all I have—all—all."

"I shall take all you have."

"You need not use violence, you shall have it all without."

"You are making but a poor use of your time," Bayley
replied, "you know what I mean. Pray if you have a prayer
to say, for in five minutes your brains will pollute that wall."

"Don't talk so, Captain Bayley, it was all a joke," he screeched, as he saw the gun raised. Had Jarrol not been a rank coward he might have seen that Bayley was nearly as helpless as himself, his legs shook under him and he was obliged to lean against the door to save himself from falling, his arms too were in such a disabled and numbed state that he could scarcely lift the gun to his shoulder. When Jarrol saw Bayley's hesitation, he hoped he had made an impression on him, and he exclaimed, " I will do anything to live—I will be your slave, I will kneel to you," and he fell upon the ground and crawled towards Bayley, whose whole frame displayed the abhorrence in which he held him.

As he continued advancing, by a great effort Bayley gave the abject coward a kick in the face which sent him reeling backwards. As soon as he recovered himself, he said, " Punish me in any way you will, but don't kill me : I can't die yet."

"There is only one minute left for you to prepare," said Bayley, " and you shall die.—Waste no more breath, for your time is fast passing," and he raised the gun and kept it to his shoulder, for he had now recovered in some measure the use of his limbs.

Jarrol looked at him for a moment, and falling on his side screamed for mercy's sake to spare him until he could pray.— " Only let me try," he said,—" only let me collect myself—and this covenant further saith—no, no, not that :—and be it further enacted—declare this to be my last will and testament—in sound health of mind and body—no—no : spare me, I can't pray yet," and he fell upon his face and lay without motion on the ground.

Bayley dropped the muzzle of the gun for the second time, as he exclaimed, " I will leave him for the hangman, but I must put it out of his power to do me further mischief." He then took from his knapsack a pair of handcuffs and fastened them on Jarrol's wrists, after which he bound him to a heavy log which Dodge used for a seat, and departed from the hut, leaving him to his fate.

"There's no place like home," said Dodge, as he kicked open the door of his hut with such energy that it bid fair to smash the novel hinges. "Thunder! why what's here?" he said, advancing on the bushranger, whose countenance, changed as it was, he soon recognised. Stationing himself in the doorway, he shouted to his companions, "Come on and see an original babe in the wood.—Ho! ho!! flattered by the honor of your visit, Mr. Jarrol, or Barrell, or what your name is." But Jarrol was in an exhausted state and uttered only a low moaning. It seemed as if the bushranger was again in the power of those most interested in his capture only to create disappointment. After he had been liberated from the terrible position in which Bayley left him, with the miserable prospect of being either starved, or delivered into the power of the law, and had partaken sparingly of some food, he partially revived, but his mind wandered, and when he spoke it was of things and places far away. It became evident that the terror he had experienced had overthrown his reason. Occasional fits of frenzy were followed by great depression. An attempt was made (but without success) to relieve him of the handcuffs in which it will be remembered Bayley left him. Whilst those in the hut were engaged with the bushranger, the dog Lady appeared upon the scene. She entered the hut with a growl, and evinced anything but a friendly feeling towards Jarrol, and at last the attentions she paid were of such a decidedly hostile nature, that Dodge was induced to order her to keep at a more respectful distance. "Now I know all about it," he said, talking to his dog, who continued growling, "this fellow served you very badly, but you see he has since been served worse

T

himself, that must be your revenge, so lay down." Obedient
to her master's word Lady reluctantly complied, but in such a
position that every action of the bushranger was under her observation.

As Dodge was endeavouring to force a little spirit into the
mouth of the gasping man, he shrieked, "Poison! poison!
—hellfire! poison!—poison me, what for?—I'm nothing—I'm
a ——— what am I?" As Hugh Raymond was stooping
over, Jarrol fixed his eyes upon him in a peculiarly earnest
manner and momentarily recognised him. Transient as was
the impulse given, it was sufficiently lasting to bend Jarrol's
wandering thoughts in the direction so much desired. Drawing Hugh towards him with his manacled hands he whispered
"Don't marry her, she is a beggar: I made her so years and
years ago.—I tell you Annie Raymond is a beggar." Hugh
and Slinger looked on but remained silent, hoping that in his
wanderings some useful information might unwittingly escape
him; but a long season of incoherency gave place to a morose
silence. They were beginning to despair, and were whispering together, when Jarrol, looking hard at them, cried out
"It's a lie—a conspiracy, you are plotting against me; the
deeds were not put there by me, but they are safe, very safe.—
There, open the pannel.—So, so, as I left it. Now look beyond.—Open that one, the deeds are there, but you can't touch
them, they belong to my son—*she* is his wife, and so Master
Hugh Raymond see to what your plotting has come at last.—
Ha! ha!!" Slinger carefully noted on paper every word as it
fell from the bushranger's lips, and when he ceased speaking,
turned to Dodge. Although nothing was said, Dodge nodded
his head mysteriously, and remarked, that it was "a subject
requiring to be well smoked over" before he could venture to
give an opinion worth anything.—"The deeds and the pannel!

I say, friend," he said, abruptly turning to Raymond, "are you fond of long voyages? because, my impression is, that from what little you have imparted to me of your connection with this respectable gentleman a visit to England might be a good speculation for you just now." This was a matter which had not been altogether unthought of by Hugh, but the subject at that time was pursued no further.

The evening grew on apace, and as the light of day died out, the bushranger became more silent and composed. He was laid in a corner of the hut on a couch of leaves. After the friends had discussed in whispers what course they should pursue towards their prisoner and had partaken of the cheer which the store in the chimney afforded, they made a shakedown, intending to keep watch and watch during the night. Whether it was that having a roof once more over their heads acted as a soporific, or that the contents of the "poison" bottles had an unusually soothing effect, it is very certain that the first watchman fell asleep without inconveniencing himself by waiting to be relieved, nor was it till the morning sun shone brightly through a hundred crevices in the hut that they woke and were not a little astonished to find Jarrol gone, and Lady occupying his place. Dodge rubbed his eyes very hard indeed: "We are saved some trouble at least," he said, "for our prisoner has disposed of himself. So much the better. Lady come here. Where is he?" Lady appeared thoughtful. "Show him then." Lady went to the door, so did Dodge. The door was opened, and the dog looking up in her master's face trotted off in the direction of the creek. Arrived on its banks, there, sure enough, were the fresh impressions of human feet. Glancing in the direction where he kept his boat he saw her laying just as he had left her. Then he walked for some distance both up and down the creek, but failed to discover any other tracks on either side but those to which Lady had first conducted him, and which led into the water. It was very clear that whoever might have left them had neither returned or reached the opposite bank.

"I thought he was born to be hanged," Dodge muttered, after musing for a minute or two : "I was wrong. Lady come here, keep dark, say nothing about it, he is gone—down," pointing with his finger, "and I hope he will stop there." This was not altogether an unnatural wish, for Dodge expected that his acquaintances would leave in the course of a few days, and the prospect of a drowned body floating about in his neighbourhood was not by any means suggestive of pleasant associations.

He had turned his face towards the hut when Raymond and Slinger joined him, and instantly comprehending the motive which had drawn him in the direction of the water, inquired if he had seen anything of Jarrol.

"No," he replied, "nothing: but I have a notion he might be found if we had grapling irons : Lady and I consider that he walked *into* the water, but we can't find that he ever came *out* again."

They returned and were examining the remaining evidences in the mud, when a horseman was seen approaching from the opposite plain, and he was soon brought up by the creek. To the usual inquiry of " What news ? " his reply savoured strongly of the bush. " Bad enough ; baccy's scarce, and I hear the bushrangers are out.—You can't lend me a pipe of tobacco, can you, mates ? "

" With all my heart," said Dodge. Steady, I'll chuck it across, unless you would like to come over and breakfast with us."

The new arrival not liking to risk the loss of the tobacco in its transit, tethered his horse, and was deliberately preparing to swim the stream, when he was prevented by Dodge, who slid his boat into the water from behind the mangrove trees and brought the stranger across by a more convenient method.

"So you have heard that bushrangers are about, have you?" said Dodge, after his passenger was landed and his pipe in full operation. We need hardly say the reply was looked forward to with some anxiety by all.

"Now I'll tell you all about it. You see I am out for stray cattle; and this morning, just arder I'd started, who should I come across but Rugsby's Jack—his stockman, you know; and, says he, 'Why, Blaizes, is that you?' (they call me Blaizes," he said, parenthetically, because I got my freedom for assisting at a large fire in Sydney and saving a life or two.) 'Have you got any baccy?' says he. 'A pipe or two,' says I. 'I'm starving,' says he, 'for want of a smoke. I was cleaned out of my baccy t'other day by bushrangers; they meets me, bails me up, as if I'd been a gentleman, cleans out my pouch and every blessed pocket I've got, they did'nt leave me a grain; and here I am destitute, an absolute beggar. You haven't another pipefull to spare me?' Well I could not refuse, and so that's how I'm scarce o'baccy, and how I come to know the bushrangers are out. Rugsby's people is expecting a visit from 'em, and I'm just going to skirt the scrubs for cattle, and call at the head station on my way back."

"Rugsby is a trump," said Dodge, "and if it was not that my companions might object to it, I'd take a short cut across the country myself."

But the friends consented without hesitation to accompany him wherever he might be disposed to lead them, and added, that they expected to find in Rugsby an old colonial acquaintance. So the few preparations necessary were hurriedly made; some scraps of lead found lining an old tea-chest were melted down and cast into bullets, and as more were required, a quantity of shot, which Dodge had in store, was also converted into a similar use.

"Shot," Dodge said, "was, in a general way, the sort of metal to fill the pot with, but bullets will do for that as well as other things, and we are not going foraging for a dinner to day."

CHAPTER XIII.

As Rugsby's station lay in the direction of Melbourne, the two partners took a farewell look at the hut as they were about leaving, and availed themselves of the opportunity to thank its owner warmly for the hearty welcome and valuable assistance he had rendered them in their search for a station.

"No thanks, no thanks," was the reply; "I never enjoyed a trip more in my life. We have been very lucky too. Many men have been bushing it for years and have not seen such adventures, nor learnt as much as you have, during the short time we've been together. To those who don't understand it, the bush is of all other places the most miserable, outlandish, and monotonous; but I think you will acknowledge that it possesses some novelties and excitements. Of course, a man who spends one month in building a hut, and then is satisfied to vegetate in it for the remainder of his life, is not one who should have chosen the bush for a home. He," Dodge said, with some show of contempt, "should have been satisfied to remain a 'respectable' man in some old settled country: his quiet habits and respectability are out of place in the bush. I don't like a man who is all work neither. Your natural historian now, one who employs himself all day in poking nameless beetles out of holes and from under the bark of trees, hunting up new facts and observing all sorts of strange things, though he would never make a fortune, is a sort of man that one can put up with. In fact, I once had a weakness that way myself, and actually was credulous enough to fancy I had discovered a new animal, gave it a name (after myself of course), but the conceit was taken out of me when I found that it had been described over and over again and christened years before. The right sort to go-a-head here are just the men who would do as well anywhere else, perhaps better. Now I should say you two would find the bush a profitable and pleasant life. To me it is the latter certainly, not the former; why, I can't exactly say but I have a notion that if such things as bills and money, and debts, and lawyers, and such like had been unknown, I might have done very well. I have a great notion of selling myself up to save the lawyers trouble, and going shepherding or stock keeping, or any other equally gentlemanly occupation."

"At what wages?" Slinger inquired jokingly.

"Money no consideration whatever," was the reply: "a comfortable home and pleasant companions, every thing found, liberal rations, unlimited tobacco, no grog, as much work as you like, and just enough money to cover an annual spree in town, and I'm your man. I can do all sorts of bush work, splitting and fencing, carpentering, clearing, grubbing, ploughing, in fact, there's nothing a bushman ought to be able to do that I cannot do.—Try me."

Dodge appeared so very much in earnest that after consulting with Raymond, Slinger proposed to purchase his cattle and to engage his services forthwith. Dodge acquiesced readily, and the bargain was soon completed.   Long before Ruffin's station was reached it was arranged that on his return Dodge should possess himself of the newly discovered station, whilst the partners should lose no time in procuring the necessary squatting license from the Commissioner of Crown lands.

"But perhaps," said Slinger, "you would like to come to town with us; you can stop at our store if you please, we will give you as warm a welcome there as you have us in the bush."

"Oh no, thank you," said Dodge, "too many duns and lawyers there for me.   I wish they were as scarce in the woods as bushrangers are in the town, although I have heard of some instances where even they could not resist the temptation of leaving their solitary life though at great risk.   A few years ago there was a fellow in Van Dieman's Land who kept the whole island in terror by his daring acts, and there was a heavy figure set upon him.   There was a large ball given at Government House to which all the big-wigs, many officers, and the most respectable merchants were invited.   By some means the fellow was introduced as a gentleman just arrived from England, and on the company assembling he became quite the lion of the room—a roarer, and no mistake.   All the women were fascinated by his bearing and conversation, the men on the contrary voted him quite a bore.   On breaking up, the Governor's Lady very graciously expressed a wish that he would visit Government House frequently during his stay in Hobarton, in which request her husband joined.   He thanked them for the honor they had done him, but regretted that circumstances over which he had no control would oblige him to leave town immediately, and thus prevent his availing himself of the kind invitation.   Her ladyship was rather curious to know what he was in such a hurry to leave for.   'Your ladyship,' he said

playfully, ' can keep a secret, I suppose.' Her ladyship could.
' May I exact a promise from your ladyship that you will not divulge that of which I am about to inform you until three days
have elapsed,' he said, smiling blandly on her. ' Mine is a
romantic story,' he added. ' I cannot refuse a request made
with such a grace : upon my honor I will not divulge your secret. Are you satisfied ?' ' I am. The reason then, madam,
of my hasty flight is simply this, there is a reward of £500 upon my head—don't start, madam, or we shall be observed, and
the neighbourhood of Hobarton is rather a dangerous place
for Kangaroo Jack the bushranger to reside in, therefore I have
the honor of wishing your ladyship a very good night and pleasant dreams.' The Governor's wife was true to her word, and
the bushranger was not taken for several years afterwards."

"Listen!" Dodge exclaimed, coming to a sudden halt,
" I thought I heard a shot fired : yes, and there is another—
we shall soon be at Rugsby's." As they proceeded five or six
shots were heard in rapid succession. " I tell you what it is,
lads, let us look to our arms : it isn't sporting they are, and it
strikes me; unlike friends in many cases, we have arrived at
the right time. Now then, my boys, don't you smell the powder? quick march ;" and they all set off at a round pace, which
soon brought them in sight of the buildings comprising Rugsby's
head station. The largest was a long slab built and bark roofed
hut, having two windows and a door, all situated in front. It
stood on the slope of a hill from which the trees had been
partly cleared; and at no great distance was a log house which
served as a store, having a door only, a narrow space left
between two slabs was the substitute for a window. From
the shelter of the trees nearest the huts, figures were seen partially to emerge and after firing an occasional shot, they fell
back into their old positions. One more adventurous or fool-

U

hardy than the rest rushed from his concealment and made a dash for a tree standing a few yards in advance of his former position ; it was only the work of a few seconds, but four shots from the occupiers of the principal building was a significant proof that keen eyes were watching the motions of those who evidently formed the attacking party.

"I see how it is," said Dodge, after a few minutes' consideration, 'tis the bushrangers sure enough, they have taken the hut and have been surprised in it by some people in pursuit of them ; it will be a considerable tough job too to turn them out of their quarters."

A tall man now came towards them under shelter of the trees, and the surprise of Hugh and Slinger was great when they discovered in him their fellow passenger, Big Mick. As soon as he recognised them he dropped his gun, seized Hugh by the hand, and danced about wildly in the exuberance of his joy, whooping in such a strange fashion that Dodge stood with his finger upon the trigger of his gun in a state of uncertainty whether he ought not to make use of his weapon without delay · he was soon set right on this point. A bullet from the hut warned them they were observed · it came whistling by and buried itself deeply in a log some distance beyond them. " Sure, my dear gentlemen," were the first intelligible words Mick uttered, after they had all sought shelter behind a large gum tree, " but you are come at the lucky moment, just in time to see all the divelment and fun going on.—Ah! good morning, Mr. Dodge,—you here too ? "

" Yes," said Dodge, " here I am ; how is your master, and what's the row—bushrangers, Eh ? "

" You may say that : them blackguards," Mick replied, with a jerk of his head towards the hut, " have been bothering the neighbourhood lately, and I just heard this morning there

was a party in search of them, and so as I hadn't been in a
scrimmage for a long while, niver since I left dear ould Ireland,
I told my wife I was going to look for wild cattle, and by the
powers I've found 'em. As for my Masther, Misther Ruffin,
he's here somewhere, and wont he enjoy himself by and by."
During the conversation, the owner of the station joined them,
but he carried no weapon. After mutual recognitions, Dodge
inquired the reason.

"Reason enough," he replied in rather a surly tone, "all
my arms are in possession of the fellows who now occupy my
place yonder. Ruffin and some friends called on me this
morning to ask my aid in an endeavour to take the bushrangers. I had agreed, we had made all arrangements and were
sat down to a comfortable breakfast, when, before you could say
Jack Robbinson, d——e *if they hadn't taken us*. There were
ten, all mounted, one of 'em on my own horse, and they rushed the hut. Unfortunately, all our arms had been piled outside,
ready for a start, and when I had reached the door expecting to
find some fellows come to join us, I was met by an ugly-looking
brute who poked the muzzle of a pistol in my face and inquired
whether I could take a hint. 'We don't want to hurt any
one,' he said, ' but we mean to stock ourselves with provisions,
that's all. What we have to do, we wish done without bloodshed; that's all I have to say, so hold my horse.'

"Your horse," said I, " why its mine."

"'Come, no grumbling,' he replied, as he glanced to one
of his gang who stood a few paces from the door. I was mightily inclined to mount as I took the bridle from his hand, but I
didn't care to leave my companions in a fix. They fared no
better than myself. One of them who ventured to make some
show of resistance with a carving knife, was unceremoniously
knocked down with the but end of a pistol, and the rest were

huddled up in a corner, in which position they were kept by the table being placed in front of them.—The hut was ransacked and every thing turned topsy-turvey. The only decent coat I possessed was appropriated, and one of my two linen shirts went for tinder. After they had laden their horses with provisions from my store, the rascals added insult to injury, for they set to and ate up all the breakfast I had prepared for my friends. In rummaging out my stock they had come across some rum, the remnant of my last spree, and I was in hopes they would have drank freely, but the one who appeared to be the leader of the gang seized upon the liquor immediately it was produced, and serving out a small portion to each of his comrades, he spilt the remainder upon the ground. Although this proceeding was evidently distasteful, no one ventured to remonstrate. I was now ordered to go inside and to assist in tying my friends together by the arms in order to prevent the possibility of pursuit, but this I positively refused to do. All the bushrangers were in the hut, and the horses with their burdens hitched up outside, when we were startled by a rattling volley followed by a loud cheer. All was confusion, and in the midst of it I and my friends made a bolt, rushed outside, holding up both hands to show we were unarmed, and nearly had our brains kicked out, for two horses were struggling in the doorway in the agonies of death. The bushrangers also endeavoured to escape, but finding it hopeless, they returned to the hut, and from all I can judge they mean to fight it out; the rope is about their necks and they know it. All this accounts for your seeing me unarmed, but though there are no spare weapons yet, there will be by and by, for those fellows know how to handle a rifle as well as the men who have come out to take them and who dropped upon them at such a convenient time."

During Rugsby's account of the occurrences which had led

to the present aspect of affairs, a brisk fire had been exchanged between the combatants, but no material damage had been done to either side. A shot from Dodge was quickly answered from the hut.

" You see," said Dodge to our friends, " it can't be expected that you care much about this kind of thing, but when I'm in a mess I like to be in the thick of it, so I shall take up a position where I can rake the hut and be in closer communication with the more active of the assailants." He left Raymond and Slinger, and his presence in the midst of the fray was announced to them by three cheers. As if by one consent the whole direction of the attack was placed in his hands, and he was not long in disposing the means at his command in the most advantageous manner. He drew off a number of men, and amongst them Hugh and Slinger, and stationed them under shelter of the store which commanded one end of the hut, and with these he continued more particularly to act. As the day drew on the firing from the hut grew more slack, and at last almost ceased. A council of war was held, at which a feeling prevailed, from which, however, Dodge dissented, that the time was come for making a general attack and taking the bushrangers' strong hold by storm. Dodge proposed that a parley should be held with the enemy, and since they must have become convinced that escape was almost hopeless, he trusted the affair might be settled without bloodshed. It became a question who was to be the adventurous diplomatist, and all eyes were turned on Dodge. After ordering offensive operations to cease, he silently left the assembly, and in a few moments returned with a piece of white linen tied to the end of a stick. Our readers must not be too curious to know from whence the rag was procured, but it answered the end intended admirably. After flourishing it at arm's length for a short time, Dodge roared out at the top of his by no means feeble voice, "Hut! ahoy!" and an answer was immediately returned

"Listen," he went on to say, "I am coming unarmed to explain to you the utter hopelessness of your situation, and to afford you the only chance remaining for your lives. If you deal treacherously with me, every man here will see me amply revenged; won't you, lads? A simultaneous cheer arose from all sides. With the utmost coolness, extending both arms, and still carrying the novel flag of truce, Dodge left the shelter of the store and walked towards the door of the hut, from whence a tall man issued in a similar attitude. After exchanging a few words they went back together, and the door was closed.

"You are as good as taken," were the first words Dodge uttered as he entered. "Don't deceive yourselves, you can't escape. As it is, you have shed no blood in the fray, and may escape hanging."

"But since the choice remains with us, we prefer the risk of being shot," was the rejoinder.

"Well, it's all a matter of opinion," Dodge remarked; "give me a light for my pipe." This request was complied with, and he handed his pouch to the leader of the gang, who also proceeded to smoke, and the two sat down and remained for a time silent. After scanning each other closely, Dodge said, "I like your cut vastly, and I don't fancy this is the first time we have met. Your being in the company of such very respectable gentlemen as I see about you does rather bother me. How is it?"

"I don't feel disposed to offer you any explanation upon that point," said the leader, "and I presume it is not the object of your mission. Let us proceed to business. You come to demand our surrender. We refuse. What then?"

"You are entirely in error," Dodge replied; "let us quite

understand each other. I did not come to demand your surrender, but to offer you the alternative between yielding and hanging. You have not yet absolutely refused; when you have, I can answer your last question."

" We do refuse then on any terms."

" I am very sorry for it : and now I have no difficulty in giving you the information you ask. You will be dead or prisoners before sunset. You are surrounded on all sides, and fresh men are arriving every hour. Am I to understand that you reject my offer ? "

" You are ; we know the worst that can happen to us ; but what is to prevent our keeping you a prisoner ? "

" Nothing," Dodge replied, " but this, that I put myself into your power hoping to save your lives, though at the hazard of my own."

It has been well said that even the greatest rascals have some good points in their nature which outlive the commission of crimes of the deepest die. The man who acted as leader opened the door without saying another word and motioned Dodge to depart, who returned to his friends and recounted to them the failure of his mission, when the firing recommenced.

During his absence, at Slinger's suggestion, a rough kind of shield had been constructed of split slabs capable of being borne before an advancing party. It was not long allowed to remain useless, and eventually, as will be seen, proved one of the principal agents in unhousing the bushrangers. A quantity of fibrous bark was collected from the adjacent trees and bound loosely together at the end of a stout pole, fire was set to it, and under cover of the shield of slabs, which was borne by several stout fellows, an advance was made towards the enemy's quarters amidst a general cheer; but it was of short duration, for a shot striking a defective part penetrated the shield and wounded one of the bearers badly. As soon as those stationed in front of the hut saw the occurrence they made a simultaneous rush but were met by a steady fire: every shot told, and they were obliged to fall back carrying with them several wounded comrades.

At this stage of the proceedings three mounted troopers, constituting the body-guard of a stout gentleman who was ob-served making himself very active in the background, joined in the fray, and for a time they engaged the particular attention of the enemy. The gentleman proved to be no other than Mr. Robberson, the hero of the "Big Ann." He had been dispatched to aid in the capture of the bushrangers, and quite unintentionally he had arrived upon the scene of action, but like a good general he did his utmost to keep out of harm's way. and under the friendly shelter of a grove of trees, issued orders which no one thought of obeying but the three unfortunate convict troopers who had been placed under him.*

Whilst the shield was being overhauled and strengthened, and preparations were making for a second attack under its friendly cover, one of the troopers was sent by Mr. Robberson with an order that the unwieldy machine was to be placed at his service, so that he might shift his position in safety nearer to the centre of operations. A general laugh announced the delivery of the message, and Dodge, after learning who the im-portant gentleman was from whom the command emanated, sent the bearer of it back with a polite intimation that the shield was at Mr. Robberson's service, and that he was quite at liberty to come for it. The irate magistrate was almost

---

* The ranks of the border police were usually filled by men who had been transported for military offences

beside himself when he found the contempt with which his authority was treated, and he so far forgot his natural cowardice that under the protection of his guards' horses he prepared, by a circuitous route, to demand in person the respect due to his rank. One horse was shot down in performing this service, and Mr. Robberson arrived among the picturesque group of combatants quite out of breath and in a high state of excitement, if not in absolute terror. As soon as he recovered himself, he singled out Dodge, of whom he had some previous knowledge, and addressing him by name he required to know who had dared to send such an insulting answer to his demand.

"I sent the reply," said Dodge; "but I see no great daring in the act. To be plain with you, squire, you are out of place here: go home."

"I shall represent your conduct, sir, to the authorities. It is unsafe to give men like you licences for land. You are a rebel, sir, and quite unfit to be engaged in a service of this kind. I hereby take upon myself the command. Now, men, advance and capture those villains in the hut."

"Bravo!" cried Dodge; "hooray! You are the sort of fellow for this work: active (Mr. R. was grown more corpulent than ever), energetic, bustin with dignity, and choke full of spirit and pluck.—You are the sort:—now then, show us the nearest way to the door yonder," and Dodge jostled Mr. R. from the tree, behind which, however, he again quickly retreated.

"Now really, my men," Mr. R. appealed to those who were witnesses of the scene, "this is too bad; you allow a fellow, who is no better than a low degraded outlaw, who at this moment ought to be in a jail, to insult your sovereign as represented in my person." After delivering himself thus, amidst the

x

smiles of his auditory, Mr. Robberson drew himself up to his full height (about five feet six inches), beating himself with one hand upon the breast whilst with the other he struck his hat fiercely over his brows as if he, the figurative sovereign, having had his crown recently shaken in some civil discord, was preparing to wear it at all hazards. Mr. Robberson's action, coupled with his words, had such a ludicrous effect, that the smiles of those surrounding him were lost in broad grins. These demonstrations produced anything but a soothing effect upon the excitable magistrate, who, looking round for some one on whom to vent his wrath, his eye fell on Dodge, and he forthwith fell foul of that supremely cool individual.

"This is all your doing, you Dodge · I know you. I shall remember you. You are the man that skulks from bailiffs; but I'll beat up your quarters yet. A troop of border police shall vindicate the majesty of the law before long, and rid the country of a pauper humbug."

Slinger began to grow indignant, but Dodge looked on as if it were an impossibility he could be the person alluded to: he however quietly said to a bystander, "See to the poor gentleman's head."

"Humph!" Slinger exclaimed: "a pauper, eh? Well, Mr. Robberson, it is not an uncommon thing to find men without a penny, worth their weight in gold; and others, with pockets overflowing, not worth a —— "

"Easy," Dodge said to Slinger, "I can fight my own battles. Let us drop this nonsense; we have our work before us: is every thing ready?" Every thing was ready. "Now, Mr. Robberson, who is going to transact this delicate piece of business, you or I?" The gentleman was silent: perhaps with indignation.

The shield was raised and tested, when it was pronounced

bullet proof, and was again moved out from behind the trees. This time both Hugh and Slinger accompanied Dodge; who, before starting on the doubtful service, offered the post of honor, as well as danger, to Mr. Robberson; who, however, declared that as the conduct of the affair had been taken out of his hands by force, he should decline interfering any further. A very judicious decision.

As Dodge was leaving, he offered his hand to Mr. Robberson, and exclaimed, "Come, shake it, it is far cleaner than it looks, and I don't care to leave you with any ill feeling." But Mr. Robberson was far too dignified a personage to regard Dodge's honest freedom with the respect it deserved, so he coolly turned his back upon him; whereupon a torch was again lighted, and amidst a round of cheers the advance was gallantly and rapidly made. The firing from the bushrangers almost ceased until the attacking party approached near the back of the hut. The lighted brand was then thrust under the dry bark of which the roof was constructed. As this daring exploit was being performed, repeated volleys were fired from the interstices of the slabs, and once the door was opened as if for the purpose of making a sally upon the gallant little band; the utter hopelessness, however, of such a proceeding became apparent, for those situated so as to command the front of the hut, and who were not unprepared for an emergency of the kind, poured in such a well-directed fire, that the door was quickly closed. A brisk breeze, which was laden with the sweet scent of the wattle and other bush flowers, and but ill accorded with the bloody work which now appeared imminent, aided the spread of the flames, in which one end of the hut became partially enveloped.

Those who made the successful assault had retreated about twenty yards, when an event occurred which bid fair to leave them completely exposed to their enemies. One of the cords was shot through with which the slabs of the shield were fastened, and it appeared more than probable that the whole fabric would fall to pieces; a sudden jerk, when lifted, would have been sufficient to ensure its complete destruction, and the bullets which now rattled upon it like hail, gave but too painful an illustration of the probable fate of those behind it, if deprived of its friendly shelter.

Mr. Robberson had all this time been ensconced in safety, but as there appeared a probability that the affair was growing to a climax, he occasionally ventured from his shelter for a moment to notice the turn events were taking. As the flames spread and the firing from the hut grew slack, he became proportionably valiant, and evinced a disposition to share in the conclusion of the fray, which was now evidently approaching. But an unerring eye was upon him, and a heart made callous by years of crime, misery, and degradation, was only intent in that hour of peril to consummate its deadly revenge, made doubly bitter by a sense that it was founded in wrong and injustice. Mr. Robberson had turned to give some instructions to one of his troopers, when he uttered a groan and fell forward upon his face, at the same moment a cry (it might have been of agony,) was heard to proceed from the hut and rang through the woods, mingling in the din and turmoil of the fight. The flames spread and crackled through the building, notwithstanding its defenders had succeeded in displacing parts of the roof. The capacious chimney, which carried off volumes of smoke, alone enabled them to hold their ground. To add to the confusion of the scene, the parched grass near had taken fire which spread with alarming rapidity, and many of the besiegers were forced to retreat before it. A clump of tea-tree scrub checked its progress, but only for a moment, for a breeze

sprung up and carried the flames crashing into its very centre; long shreds of bark* hanging from the trees afforded fresh food for its insatiable appetite, and many monarchs of the forest, whose age might perhaps have been reckoned by centuries, were left stricken never to revive again, whilst those which had suffered from former conflagrations continued burning fiercely after the great body of flame had passed them.

All this time the shield and those it sheltered remained stationary, but Dodge declared he could restrain himself no longer, and bidding those who chose to follow him, he prepared to make a dash for the door. At this moment a man was seen through the smoke on the top of the hut throwing down the logs which it is the fashion of bushmen to lay upon all bark roofs to prevent the heat of the sun from warping them. Slinger was following close on Dodge's heels when this figure attracted their attention, and the gun of the old bushman was already at his shoulder, when Slinger griped him by the arm and exclaimed, "Come back, there's a good fellow; for God's sake, if it be not too late, save that unfortunate man."

" What *is* up?" Dodge exclaimed; "are you growing sentimental? He is past all saving, and it is only a question now whether he dies by lead or hemp. Believe me, that fellow is not going to be taken alive."

As if to make the surmise good, the person who was the subject of conversation was seen to stagger and seek support by grasping an angle of the chimney; a cloud of smoke hid him momentarily from view, and then he fell headlong to the ground. His fall was the signal for a general rush. There was no cheering this time, and although some shots were fired upon the attacking party and several fell, the result was no longer doubtful.

* Many of the trees of Australia shed their bark and not their leaves.

The first who reached the door was Dodge, who grasping a piece of wood which had formed part of the shield, used it in the manner of a battering-ram, and so effectually that he found himself in the midst of the bushrangers in the burning hut before his friends could join him, laying about him with all his might, and roaring at the top of his voice, " You are all my prisoners." Two of his antagonists fell prostrate at his feet. A pistol was fired at him, but the ball striking the powder flask which he carried inside the breast of his flannel shirt, glanced off without injury. All this was only the work of a few moments, and when Hugh and Slinger entered they found him on his knees pummelling with his fists the poor wretch who had made the unsuccessful shot at him. The indignant bushman appeared to have quite forgotten the presence of the other men, who were paralyzed at the loss of their leader, as he roared between his blows, " So you wont surrender, eh ! and after I've taken you. I hope this will be a lesson to you."

The rest is soon told. The half stifled, but only partly subdued men, were dragged out of the building which they had defended with a bravery equalled only by the badness of their cause, and when they had been properly secured, every attention was paid to the wounded. Mr. Robberson was borne faint and speechless into the store house, and he was shortly followed by Bayley, who our readers will have recognised in the leader of the bushrangers, and whose hurts seemed very desperate.

Amongst those who had been engaged in the fray was a certain bush practitioner known as Doctor Bathey, whose acquirements were so extensive, or his vanity so egregious, that he was at all times prepared to attend cases arising amongst the settlers, their horses, cattle, or dogs; but his favorite practice was upon the human subject.

" Two very bad cases indeed," this personage remarked,

after he had felt the pulses of the wounded men; "very low—
desperately low—in fact, infernally low."

"Can nothing be done for them?" Dodge, who knew Dr.
Bathey well, inquired in a whisper.

"A great deal might if I had my instruments; but really,
when one considers that they both *must* die, perhaps it is as
well I am without them." Dodge thought so too. "You see
—What's his name? the magistrate, is as good as dead already,
and as for the other fellow, my professional skill would be
thrown away upon him, for what I saved, the law would spoil;
therefore," he concluded, "my opinion is that they had better
die quietly and comfortably.—Ten and sixpence if you please."

"And six! nothing less?" Dodge inquired with a very serious expression of face.

"Ten and six if you please. My scale of fees for advice is
moderate.—Dog, two shillings; cattle, five ditto; horse, seven
and six; man—noble man, ten and six."

"Knock off the sixpence," Dodge said, coaxingly.

"Impossible, my dear sir· you asked for my opinion; I
gave it you.—Ten and sixpence if you please."

"Exchange is no robbery," Dodge replied: I'll pay you in
your own coin." So drawing himself up with a look of great
importance, and gently tapping the side of his nose with his finger, he beckoned Dr. Bathey to his side, and still whispering said,
"In case you should ever come across me when I'm sick—now
pay attention to what I say—don't attempt your tinkering upon
me, or I'll be the death of you. That's *my* advice, for which
I charge you nothing. My opinion is, that you are a humbug,
an opinion cheap at ten and six, and so our account is squar-
ed;" so saying he took Bathey by the hand and with a quiet
sniggle told him in confidence, that he hadn't as much as seen
a half sov. for the last two years, but that if he would meet

him at his lawyer's and press his claim, some arrangement should be made.   The conversation which had been carried on half in joke and half in earnest was terminated by Bathey, who declared that the colony presented no encouragement for men of liberal education.

After the greater number of those recently engaged in the struggle had departed with their prisoners, the few who remained, amongst whom were Dodge and his two friends, prepared to spend the night in their present quarters, and to render such assistance to the wounded as circumstances permitted.

It was good to see the delicate attentions rendered to the sufferers by the old bushman.   His every word and action assorted but indifferently with the usual bluntness of his manner, and showed clearly enough that the rust of bush habits and associations had not materially affected his naturally humane and generous heart.

As night set in there was something truly solemn in the surrounding scene.   The silence which prevailed was only broken occasionally by the moans of the sufferers, made doubly touching to the watchers by the knowledge that no efficient medical aid could possibly reach them for many hours.   At intervals the crash of falling trees in the distance was heard, which had been ignited by the late fire, and their glowing embers dotted the country round for many miles.   A line of light spread along the distant horizon and showed that the fire was still unsubdued.

Neither Mr. Robberson nor Bayley had spoken since they had been brought into the hut, excepting to ask for water, which they drank eagerly.   Whilst Slinger was administering some to the bushranger, Bayley fixed his eyes upon him earnestly, and seizing his hand retained it for some time, and then motioned him to stoop that he might speak to him.   " I hoped to have escaped all this," he whispered, in broken accents, " but my fate has pursued me to the end. What devil put Robberson in my way?"

" Speak lower," Slinger whispered, " he lays near you, badly wounded."

" I know it," Bayley said, " and by my hand, would it were not so."

"Amen," Slinger ejaculated.

The word fell upon the ear of the magistrate, whose breathing became hurried and irregular. In scarcely intelligible language he begged his position might be changed. As Dodge and Raymond were performing this little service, he looked eagerly round the hut as if expecting some consolation was at hand, but the figure that met his gaze was not the one he sought.

On seeing Bayley, he raised himself a little, and stretching out his hands, exclaimed, " Take me away—anywhere;" and his quivering lips gave evidence of the mental struggle he was enduring. " Take me away, I say: take me out of this place."

" We are past hurting each other further now," said Bayley, mournfully: " it is too late for anything but mutual forgiveness: let us forget the past, if we can; but if you feel any difficulties on that score," this was said almost fiercely, " remember it was you who helped to make me what I am."

" Move me," Mr. Robberson moaned; and as his request was being complied with—" No: I can't bear it. Move *him* away out of my sight."

A fresh flow of blood from his wound left him exhausted and speechless in the arms of Dodge and Raymond, but his eyes were still fixed on Bayley, who averted his face as he whispered to Slinger, " How is it I can't look at him, and he can

Y

at me? When my eye meets his I feel like a coward; and instead of having only done an act of retribution, that I have committed a cold-blooded murder—no: not cold blooded: for it was the work only of a moment, and that moment one of desperation: and yet, for years, I have thought such a time might come." He grasped Slinger's hand in his agony, and entreated him for mercy's sake not to leave him, as he looked at Mr. Robberson and found him still gazing upon him; but the expression of those eyes was gone. they stared with a glassy, fixed, and unmeaning look, that yet struck more terror into the heart of the dying bushranger than would have the angry glare of a wild beast; he quailed, and his whole frame shuddered as he gathered himself together, uttering ejaculations which died away into a low moaning. Then the body of Robberson was removed out of the hut, for he was dead; and in a few short hours that of the bushranger lay beside it stark and stiff—death had done its work. The one, raised by fortuitous circumstances as far above the position in society for which he was qualified; as the other had sunk below his natural sphere, had found their level at last.

CHAPTER XIV.

" This is melancholy work," Dodge exclaimed, resting on his spade whilst digging a grave on the ensuing morning for the bushranger. " I have had to turn my hand to all sorts of things, but this I like the least of any. I've tried my hand at it before to day. Yes," he said, in reply to an inquiring look from Slinger, and with a trembling voice, " the last body I

buried was that of my only brother; and 'tis in a country like
this that one knows how to value a brother. We were bringing cattle over from the Sydney side not long after the road was
opened, and what with the anxiety and deprivations we underwent, poor Tom fell into a bad way with dysentery. One day,
when the poor fellow was well nigh exhausted, for we pushed
on, hoping to fall in with some men who we knew were before us, he desired me not to trouble about him, but to go
ahead with the cattle, and leave him to make the best of his
way after us. I would not have left a cur in such a fix, let
alone a true-hearted brother; so I told Tom that I would not
part from him come what would. I little thought then the
poor fellow would so soon part from me. Well, not to make
you as dismal as these thoughts do me, I'll cut my story
short. We halted for several days, but Tom grew worse and
worse, and I tried to cheer him up and to convince him and
myself that he would get over his sickness; but he always said
he should not. Well, the night he died,—poor fellow, he
was wandering a little bit,—' Giles,' said he, with a languid
smile, ' there's only two things in the world would do me any
good; one is, if I could look upon our old home in England
and grasp the hands of those dear friends who made it home—
how different from this, dear Giles; and yet I ought not to
complain whilst I see your face beside me and can feel your
faithful heart beating against my breast,—how hard it beats too ! '
The poor fellow was laying in my arms. ' Tis beating,' said I,
' with hope. Come, cheer up, we may live to return yet: but
what is the other thing you desire?' ' Let me think,' he said,
' I'm very weak here, I can scarcely draw breath,' laying his
hands upon his breast, ' give me some brandy with an egg in
it;' and it is my firm belief," Dodge said, " that he would
have been alive now could I by any possibility have gratified his

request. If he had asked me for my heart's blood he should have had it, but his last wish was as impossible to gratify as the first. He gradually sunk, and I saw all hope was gone. During that night, with no protection from the weather, for our tent was blown down, and hundreds of miles from any help, poor Tom breathed his last prayer in my arms. I never knew what misery was till then, and when I came to put the poor dear fellow into the ground and to carve his initials upon the tree under which I buried him with my own hands, I felt as if all the world was gone from me, and I wished a thousand times I could have gone to sleep beside him. This seems strange language from me, I dare say," Dodge said to Slinger, " but we shall know each other better by and by. Come, take a spell at digging whilst I make a coffin."

Before Slinger had completed the grave, Dodge, assisted by Raymond, stripped a tree of its bark (the invariable substitute for boarding in all bush work,) and then laying the body of the bushranger on one sheet placed another over, and binding all tightly together with a rope made of twisted grass, brought the body to the edge of the grave ready for interment.

" 'Twas under just such another tree as this," said Dodge, as they lowered it into the earth, " that I buried poor Tom, and in silence too; but come, lads, we must shake off the dismals." Seizing upon the spade he shovelled the earth into the grave without much ceremony or any further show of feeling; in fact, he seemed to think, what he had already displayed required some qualification, for when pressing down the last sods, he exclaimed, " There, you'll lay quiet enough, captain, though you havn't had the benefit of clergy."

Although the disposal of the dead body of the bushranger met with but little consideration, the case of the deceased magistrate was of a different character. His remains were wrapped in an opossum rug and kept in the hollow of a tree so that his friends might be afforded the opportunity of interring him elsewhere.

At the termination of the second day, Dodge, tired of inactivity, procured a bullock dray, which happened to be passing for a distant station, and emptying it of its contents was preparing to convey the body of the magistrate to Melbourne, when the arrival of a party of mounted police, who had been sent from town, relieved our friends of this self-imposed charge. Providing themselves with such stores as were at hand, they left the scene of the late fight, and not without a sense of thankfulness that it was with whole skins, when they noticed how the neighbouring trees were marked by the bullets which had been fired from the hut.

It was Dodge's intention to have put his companions upon a good line for Melbourne and then to have returned alone, but on being pressed he acknowledged that a visit to town would be a great treat to him, and that he should like to accompany them, only that it would be too much like putting his head into the lion's mouth.

"But," said Slinger, "you have forgotten your bargain with us. Your creditors will listen to terms, I'll be bound; and by allowing the purchase money of your station to go towards the liquidation of your debts, I dare say you may be cleared from your present difficulties."

"Bless your innocence," Dodge cried, laughing incredulously, "you'll never see me clear: I was born in difficulties, and I shall die in 'em."

"I'm not so sure of that," said Slinger. "Now just tell us, as near as you can, the position in which you stand."

"I'll show you," said Dodge, turning every pocket he possessed inside out. "There! without one single screw. When I have disposed of the proceeds of the sale of my cattle, I shall be the owner of exactly that in which I stand upright; but thank God," he said, " for all that my heart is sounder than my fortunes."

" Well said," cried Slinger, " I see your difficulties disappearing already."

" Do you?" said Dodge laughing; " just let me enjoy the sight too, for upon my life I see no chance of such a thing."

" What do you think of this proposition?" said Slinger, disregarding the interruption, " you shall go to Melbourne with us, call a meeting of your creditors—by the by, how many do you think you have?"

" Dear me," said Dodge thoughtfully, " how many? hundreds, I should say; thousands, perhaps; for I have had no end of lawyers' letters, and when you know to what a single one of those interesting documents sometimes leads, you can fancy the fix I'm in when I tell you that I have received a sufficient number to make a bonfire that would roast a lawyer whole."

" Well then," said Slinger, who perceived that Dodge knew little or nothing of his pecuniary affairs, " we must call your hundreds or thousands of creditors together, as the case may be, and state fairly to them your position, then we shall see if they may be disposed to come to any arrangement."

" But what becomes of my body in the mean time?" Dodge said mournfully; " they'll grab it—I know they'll grab it—the bloodthirsty ogres."

After a long argument, his scruples were at length so far overcome that he consented, not without considerable misgiving, to extend his journey to the town, and afterwards to leave his friends to watch and turn to the best account such events as might transpire.

After the usual vicissitudes of bush travelling, the dray tracks and rude bush roads became more numerous and well defined, all however tending in the same direction, and the little party knew by these indications that they were not many miles from the principal town in the settlement. If any further proof had been wanting, it might have been found in numerous printed bills affixed to the stems of conspicuous trees on the sandy line of road they occasionally followed, as it suited their convenience. Dodge seemed to derive considerable pleasure in perusing these characteristic documents, for he stopped opposite each and read every word of it.

" I can't be hurried," he said playfully to Slinger, who expressed a desire to push on; " I'm fond of literature. No one knows the value of a newspaper but a bushman—these are my newspapers. See here," and he read aloud from a large bill, headed " Impoundings.—At the Deep Creek a brindle-sided cow, R. off rump, supposed N.C. off thigh, like J.B. near thigh, blotched brand on off ribs and shoulder, hole in near ear and the other cut off, newly branded heart on forehead, has received a bullet or other wound in the near rump, now healed." " Hang me!" said Dodge, "if I can't fancy myself back again in the Southern States of America: this is just the style in which they advertise their runaway niggers." Whilst speaking, he walked round the tree to discover what news might be found there. A large bill met his eye, and in a conspicuous part of it he was greatly astonished to find his own name figuring in the very largest and reddest characters the typographical art of the country could then call to its aid. After giving a long and low whistle, he read through the bill word for word, but without attracting the attention of his friends: it ran as follows,—

BLOODY AFFRAY WITH BUSHRANGERS!
A MAGISTRATE SHOT!!

Death of BAYLEY and capture of all his GANG!!!

CHIEFLY THROUGH THE

GALLANT CONDUCT

OF

MR. GILES DODGE,
THE WESTERNPORT SQUATTER.

' A Public Meeting will be held in the Market Square, Melbourne, on Monday next, at 11 o'clock, a. m. sharp.

All those who admire native worth are respectfully requested to attend. The object in view is, that immediate steps may be taken for the presentation of a suitable testimonial to Mr. Giles Dodge. Such daring gallantry as was displayed by him on the above occasion must not be passed over unrewarded.

PRIGG SPRIGGS, MAYOR.
JOS. SLOPEOFF.
JONAS COBB.
J. NAILEM.
&c. &c. &c.

Vivat Regina.

"Here's news!" cried Dodge: "but I'm not to be caught with chaff.—I'm quite near enough to Melbourne: good bye."

Neither Hugh nor Slinger could quite comprehend the meaning Dodge wished to convey.

"It's not genuine," he said; drawing their attention to the bill, and poking Slinger in the ribs, "d'ye see that?" and he pointed out the name of his old legal antagonist, J. Nailem. —"It's a trap—of course 'tis; but I'm not caught yet.—Good bye, I'm off."

" Nonsense," said Hugh; "Is this the way you show your resolution? Here's a fellow," turning round to Slinger and pointing to Dodge, "who would face any created thing in the shape of a man, running away from a handbill, which after all I believe is genuine, at least I know that a certain Giles Dodge deserves the praise of the colonists for the part he played in the capture of the bushrangers. Come sit down, let us talk this matter over."

Accordingly the subject was fully discussed amidst volumes of tobacco smoke, and Dodge at length expressed a determination to "*chance it,* like Major Oakes did. Perhaps you never heard of the Major: well then, he was a rum old colonial magistrate who, whenever a doubtful case was brought against a convict servant, used to escape the bother of a long inquiry by delivering this invariable judgment, 'Hum! ha!! yes, give him five-and-twenty, *and chance it.* Bring up the next.'"

In due time the trio arrived on the banks of the picturesque Yarra Yarra River, a short distance above Melbourne, and here Dodge's heart completely failed him: nothing short of his companions first going into the town and inquiring into the genuineness of the bill they had seen would satisfy his scruples.

Raymond and Slinger soon found themselves in their own quarters, and on making known the share they had taken in the late affray, were soon crowded upon by numbers of their townsmen, all eager to get some genuine intelligence about the late stirring event. Conspicuous among them was Mr. Nailem, and on the name of Dodge being mentioned, he spoke in enthusiastic terms of the nerve and spirit he had displayed. Such an opportunity was not to be let slip, and the two friends being quite convinced that Dodge might make his appearance with perfect security, Mr. Nailem was informed of the proxi-

z

mity of his late slippery client, whereupon he declared he would
head a party to bring the hero into the town in triumph, and
that he thereupon absolved Dodge from all old scores, and called
upon those about him to note his words in order that they
might become legally binding.

A party was formed on the spot, and about thirty set off,
who were, however, joined by many others on their way. The
Yarra was crossed in the punt, and in a little while Dodge
was seen reclining in the shade of the tree under which his
friends had so lately parted from him. The fatigues of the
journey had overcome him and he had fallen sound asleep, nor
did he recover his consciousness until a loud cheer was set up.
Jumping upon his feet and rubbing his eyes, the first object
they encountered was Mr. Nailem.

Giving himself no time for consideration, he took a short
run and plunged headlong into the river. He only turned to
look at his old enemy after reaching the opposite bank. " So
you thought you'd caught me asleep, eh, Mr. N., regularly
jammed up, but I'll make tracks that you can't follow." He was
showing a clean pair of heels, when Raymond and Slinger singled themselves from the crowd and, amidst shouts and immo-
derate laughter, succeeded in making him understand the motives which had induced Mr. Nailem and others of the party to
seek him in his lurking place.

" Come, come," cried Slinger, " when *we* tell you no harm
is intended, that is sufficient."

Dodge seemed to think it so, for he recrossed the river, and
notwithstanding his dripping state, was received with open arms
by his enthusiastic admirers. His hand was grasped so hard
by Mr. Nailem that his old fears began to disturb him,
but they were of short duration, for on arriving at the punt a
crowd was waiting, and the moment he appeared they forcibly

took possession of his person, and hoisting him upon their
shoulders bore him off to the principal inn amidst the shouts
of the multitude.   There he was soon waited upon by numbers
of the townspeople, whilst those who could not gain admission
became momentarily more excited, and at last, instigated by
Nailem, they insisted that Dodge should show himself at the
window and make a speech.   Dodge remonstrated: he had never
made such an ass of himself in all his life—he couldn't do it—
he had nothing to talk about; but the crowd were inexorable,
they would hear their hero-for-the-day speak.

     " Well then," Dodge cried at last, " here goes ! "   His
appearance at the window was the signal for more cheering and
more enthusiasm.   He commenced his oration by ejaculating
short sentences by no means complimentary to the assemblage
he was addressing; he tossed his arms about wildly, and his
language became quite incomprehensible even to those near
him; but the auditors had made up their minds to be pleased,
and his task for a time was an easy one.   After many frantic
appeals for silence had been made, Dodge found himself in that
unenviable position of being surrounded by listeners without
the most remote idea of what to say to them; but if he was
nonplused for a moment, his self-possession soon came to his
aid.—"As I remarked to you before, gentlemen, after giving
you a full, true, and particular account of the whole matter
which has brought me before you, which, by the bye, I dare say
you didn't hear for the row you made, but that I could not
help (great cheering)—as I remarked to you before, under the
circumstances just named, it is the part of a good citizen to
respect the laws of his country," and then in an aside to those
nearest him, " particularly when such respect does not interfere with his personal liberty; but, gentlemen, whilst we respect the laws, we may hold whatever opinions we please about

the lawyers. For myself," he said, turning round and laying his hand on Mr. Nailem's shoulder, " I think I have found to day one of the right sort, and there may be others.   With your kind permission I will introduce to your notice our respected friend, who is more used to talking than I am;" but shouts arose—" we won't hear him—give us some more."   " I propose, then," said Dodge, who found the attention of the populace too great for his convenience,—"I propose three cheers for our country, and," he added, on second thoughts, " with nine times nine afterwards." These were accordingly given, and when the hubbub had subsided, he continued, " This is a glorious country, gentlemen." And then he folded his arms as if waiting for some one to dispute the proposition.   This resource failing, he proceeded, " True we have not a flag yet that we can call our own, (groans) but we have the happiness to live under the protection of one that will never fail us at a pinch, and one moreover that we are not called on to keep clean nor to darn when ragged, two plaguey expensive items in the expenditure of independent states.   True, our revenue does not go in the right channels (groans.)—(' I say,' he said to Slinger, who stood by, ' where the devil does it go?'   ' Where it should not, of course,' was the reply, ' none of it flows into your pocket nor mine').—There is no question about it whatever then gentlemen; our revenue is *not* expended as it should be; but as many of us don't contribute much towards it, we wont consider the subject too closely," and with such irrelevant and unconnected matter Dodge amused his auditory. During his speech he had refreshed himself so frequently by swallowing sundry glasses of liquor, which were eagerly proffered whenever a cheer from the mob afforded opportunity for a momentary pause, that the effects of the unusual libations began to tell upon him.

" Now I'm going to wind up with something crushing,"
he stammered out, in reply to an imploring look from Raymond. Turning up his sleeves and untying his neck-handker-
chief, as preliminaries, he delivered himself as follows, " I will
not detain you long, gentlemen, though I find my ideas are
crowding upon me with greater rapidity than I can find language to give them utterance. Australia Felix, like her native
gum trees, may be torn by the tempest, shaken by the thunder,
blasted by blue lightning, but it's my opinion, that all attempts
to check her progress will be vain, whilst we, her sons, continue to respect her laws and enforce obedience to them both by
our actions and example." (a laugh, and cheers.) Two or three
of his friends now endeavoured to drag him back from the window, but he shook them off, mounted on the wooden balus-
trade, and swaying himself to and fro, cried, " If any one
attempts to touch me I'll throw myself into the arms of my
friends below.—Talk! I'll talk with any man alive for £50,
not excepting that 'spectable old trump Nailem! Who'll try
me—whar's the man?" As no champion appeared upon the
lists, Dodge quietly resigned himself into the custody of his
friends, with an intimation that he was "quite unaccustomed to
public drinking, and that his feelings were beyond expression,"
which was certainly not the case with his countenance, for that
bore most unmistakable characteristics of inebriety.

We regret to have to record it, but the helpless hero was
forthwith taken to bed, from which, however, he insisted the
sheets should be first drawn, as he could not stand damp. The
extreme care he manifested for his health on this particular occasion, considering that he slept as often upon the earth as any
where else, could only be accounted for from the peculiarly ob-
livious state of his mental faculties.

A Subscription on behalf of the testimonial fund was forthwith opened, and in a few days, such was the enthusiasm of the townspeople, large sums were contributed, and every thing bid fair, under the disinterested management of the partners, for a speedy and satisfactory arrangement being made with Dodge's creditors.

A week or two in town passed away pleasantly enough, in which our two friends found ample occupation, when not engaged on their own business, (transacted during their absence by a faithful store-keeper,) in arranging Dodge's affairs. These were not found to be in so desperate a state as they had been led to anticipate. Their great difficulty consisted in inducing the old bushman to afford some slight personal attention to the matter, but he repeatedly declared that he knew nothing whatever about it, and that if they would excuse him and allow him to get a few necessary things together for the formation of the new station he should take it kindly. He had magnified his embarrassments so enormously, and was so painfully impressed with the idea that unheard of sums of money would be demanded, that his friends listened to his entreaties, and deputed him to look out, amongst other things, for a dray and some working bullocks.

The eventful day at last arrived for the presentation of the testimonial, and of course a public dinner afforded the most pleasant medium, but when Dodge found himself amongst the guests " the observed of all observers," he declared in a whisper to Slinger, that " taking bushrangers was nothing to it." After much entreaty he had consented to appear in a stiff collar and a dress coat, and although this arrangement was quite consistent with the propriety of the occasion, it was very far from conducing to his sense of ease and comfort: he had, however, taken the precaution to bring a bundle with him to the inn containing his usual habiliments.

The dinner was disposed of as most good dinners are, but perhaps, the passing of the wine afterwards was rather more rapid than would be considered strictly proper amongst slower communities;—our readers will not, therefore, be surprised to learn, when the chairman, Mr. Nailem, exposing the full front of his capacious waistcoat, slowly rose and in an impressive manner proposed long life and prosperity to their intrepid guest, Giles Dodge,—and spoke of that guest's devotion to the cause of order, and of the bravery he had evinced in ridding the country of internal foes (interpreted by Dodge into 'infernal foes),' that the toast was received with particularly loud and continuous cheering; but when, endeavouring to raise a silver salver overflowing with gold, and failing in the attempt, he almost supplicated Mr. Dodge to accept *that* as but an imperfect proof of the estimation in which his late never-to-be-forgotten and heroic conduct was held by his brother colonists—the excitement knew no bounds. One enthusiastic settler, who was well acquainted with Dodge, and it spoke volumes in his (the latter gentleman's) favor, was so far transported by the intensity of his admiration, that he swept the table near him of every movable, and requested, as a special favor, that some one present would assert that Dodge was not worth any two men in the whole settlement, the Governor and himself not excluded. As there appeared an indisposition to indulge this eccentric request, he retired under the table in a state of unmitigated disgust and wine.

The attention of the guests having been with difficulty again secured, the chairman proceeded to say, that it afforded him infinite satisfaction, and he was quite sure he might also include his respected friend, Mr. Dodge, to be able to state—and he had no delicacy in doing so, for Mr. Dodge was too honest a man to feel ashamed of the truth—that the handsome manner

in which the colonists had come forward would completely relieve Mr. Dodge from all his embarrassments, and leave him a
considerable balance afterwards.

At this information, no one was more astonished than the
person chiefly interested. He looked inquiringly at Slinger,
who simply said " Fact! Raymond and I made out the balance
sheet." Whereupon Dodge, extending a hand to each, said,
in a faltering voice, " I may thank you for all this ; " and beg-
ing the company to excuse his absence for a few minutes, he
left the room. When he returned again he was looking more
like himself, for he had doffed the dress coat and collar, and
once more appeared clothed in his usual manner.

" There," he cried, on reaching his friends, " now *I am*
happy. That confounded swallow-tail and cut-throat collar
were sufficient to alloy felicity even greater than mine. And so
I'm out of debt! I can't realize it all at once though, my
mind aint capacious enough."

It was now hinted to Dodge that the time was arrived for
him to address the company. He was rather confused at his
novel position and unconsciously commenced taking the wire
from the neck of a champagne bottle which stood near him.
Jumping on his legs with a jerk, he cried out, "A capital
notion! now look here, gentlemen, here is a bit of wire straight
as a tea-tree pole," holding it before them after the manner of
a professor of the art of legerdemain, " now observe," he said,
binding it round his finger and again holding it up for inspec-
tion, " the same piece of wire twisted and made corkscrew
fashion. Now hark'e, how shall I express the little I am bound
to, both by gratitude and inclination? shall I say it straight forward and right off, or give it a tarnation twisting? " Here he
was interrupted by loud cries of " Short and sweet."

" Well, then," said Dodge, " so it shall be. I thank you

with all my heart for the generous manner you have thought fit
to signify your approval of my poor services; but when you
come to talk of my courage, I know very well there is not a
man in this room but would have acted precisely as I did under the like circumstances. I can only further say, that if any
of you ever come across my new quarters, there you will find a
bushman's welcome, and, if you prefer it," glancing towards
the salver, "I'll serve up your mutton on a silver dish. Now I
ain't going to make a fool of myself as I did at the inn t'other
day, and down I go like poor old Pidgeon the Darkey." Here
Dodge pitched himself into his seat, and after the cheering had
subsided, he was requested to enlighten his audience respecting
his allusion to Black Pidgeon.

"Ah," Dodge said, squaring himself and drinking a glass
or two of wine, "it ain't a very lively after-dinner yarn, there's
too much water in it. I happened to be in the neighbourhood
of Port Philip Heads when the ' William Salthouse,' on entering, struck on a reef and went down. She had lots of good
stuff aboard her, and 'twas a cruel temptation to the few settlers who then lived on the borders of the bay, when they went
out for a fishing cruise, to see down below 'em (for the water
was mostly as clear as crystal,) so many good casks of liquor
all ready for tapping. Many attempts were made to raise some,
but they all failed; and at last an ingenious friend of mine,
who could turn his hand to anything, made a kind of gigantic
auger which was infallibly to do the business; but the sands
about the vessel were a favorite cruising ground for sharks,
and as them cattle don't stand on much ceremony, it was a
long time before he could make up his mind to trust himself
amongst them. However, one clear day we went off together,
and there below us lay the best bait you can set for a bushman.
No sharks were to be seen, and down went my friend armed

AA

with his auger and with a rope round his body to enable me to haul him up in case of any sharks heaving in sight before he might have time to fasten.   Well, after nearly exhausting himself to no purpose, he gave it up as a bad job, and we pulled ashore, and on getting to his hut found Black Pidgeon there.   'I've got it,' cried my friend,' that's the man to do it. Come here Pidgeon.   Are you fond of rum?'   'Berry.'   'And baccy?'   'Berry.'   'Can you dive well, Pidgeon?'   'Berry.' 'Are you afraid of *tallon-arron*?' (i. e. sharks.)   'No.'   So the poor fellow was forthwith taken into the service, and when he was shown the casks and informed they were filled with rum, his eyes glistened like a wild cat's.   'Ky!' he said, 'black fellow get berry drunk by and by, like white fellow.' Providing himself with several pieces of wood from six to twelve inches in length, sharp at both ends, and sticking a hunting knife in the band worn round his head, in less time than I have taken to tell you, he had firmly fastened the auger with the rope attached into one of the casks, which was soon weighed and safely stowed in the bottom of the boat.   Pidgeon was very anxious to lose no time in tasting its contents, but this would not do; so he went down secondly under a promise that if we got up another he should have a week's drunk. Whilst engaged with the auger a shark made bold to show him his teeth.   As quick as thought Pidgeon plunged one of the pointed sticks into his open jaws, and the shark sheered off with his mouth distended, having got more for a meal than he bargained for.   Nothing daunted, after breathing himself, the black went down again, and gave the signal to haul up.   After lifting a bit, the rope suddenly slackened, and we could feel that something had given way, and Pidgeon didn't come up as we expected.   A few bubbles rising on the surface attracted our instant attention, and on looking steadily below there was

poor old Pidgeon jammed between two casks. We both dived
for him, but he was too firmly fixed and already past our help.
The sharks soon finished him, and 'twas an ugly sight to see.
And now, having spun my yarn, with too much truth in
it, by the by, you may easily apply it. You see Pidgeon went
down and nothing could get him on his legs again : just my
case to night. But if you will allow me, as I have a decided
objection to stopping the bottle, I will give you a toast which
you will please to drink in solemn silence—' To the immortal
memory of poor old Pidgeon the Darkey.' "

At this peculiarly unfortunate moment, the enthusiastic
gentleman who, it will be remembered, retired beneath the table early in the evening, recovering his consciousness, and hearing a toast proposed (the subject was quite of secondary consideration to him), struck up at the top of his voice "For he's a
jolly good fellow." A few cries of "Turn him out," were
soon drowned by the majority of the assembly, who improved
the opportunity by chiming in with the chorus, and exhausting
a little of their superfluous excitement.

" Solemn silence, if you please, gentlemen," roared the chairman, thumping the table with such energy as to set the gold in
the salver chinking. The more the chairman exerted his authority, the less attention was paid to him, so like a sensible
man he relinquished his post, and his voice was soon heard in
the chorus raised to as high a pitch as his neighbours. But
the same words to the same tune repeated over and over again
became monotonous, so the company, by easy gradations, changed both. "He's a jolly good fellow" gradually developed
itself into "We won't go home till morning," and that popu-
lar matutinal song was transformed into something else. The
finale was made up of everything in part and nothing in parti-

cular, for each guest indulged in his favorite ditty to his own measure.

" The best friends must part . " and Dodge, with Raymond and Slinger, who had contrived to preserve a respectable state of sobriety, prepared to take their leave.

" Good night, Dodge—good night, old boy," Ruffin said to him ; " mind how you navigate home with all that rhino in your pockets. Steer a straight course. I'd take care of you, only I'm thinking somebody else would have to look for me afterwards.—The weather is foggy, very."

" Talk of navigation," said Dodge, " Did you ever hear me spin the yarn of old Jock Lurcher's proficiency in the art? "

" No."

" Then I'll tell it.—Shall I tell it? " he said, looking round.

An universal assent was given by all who were capable of signifying as much.

" Jock Lurcher, then, lads, once sailed in the ' Teazer,' a very tidy craft, which is more than any one ever said of her skipper when they really came to know him, for he was an unmitigated brute. When in harbour his vessel was the picture of neatness; and although his men were hard worked, they did their duty with a will, for the captain was as amiable to them as a sucking dove. His passengers and their visitors were treated like princes—nothing was too good for them. The very choicest wine was at their service, and there was no stint of anything; but the captain was moderate in all things. Those who didn't know him would say, ' that Lurcher is something of a captain, so kind and considerate to his men, so humane to his passengers; it must be quite a treat to go a voyage with him.' The consequence was, that where he was not known he was never at a loss to obtain his full complement of passengers.

He was just the fellow a romantic emigrant should have gone the voyage with: and then he was a decidedly pious man too, he couldn't abide swearing aboard his ship. This was Jock Lurcher at anchor. Now we will get him out of harbour and let him be fairly afloat. How he would curse then, to be sure! His passengers were stinted in everything, even in the execrable wine provided for their use. Of course, with so nice a fellow they had made no special agreement as to rations, nor anything else, previously to engaging their berths. Woe betide the rash man who ventured to remonstrate.

" ' Sir,' would have been his reply, ' you want to raise a mutiny on board, do you? but by ———— I'll have you put in irons and gagged, sir, I will, if I hear another disrespectful word; ' and then turning upon his heel, ' I've got you on blue water now, and if you don't like my ship you can leave her, there's lots of room outside.' This fellow was once making the home passage round the Horn, and as he'd been drunk ever since he left port, something like a month, and would insist on navigating the ship in his own way, you may judge pretty well that he got rather out of his reckoning. When he should have been getting into warmer latitudes, the weather became colder and colder every day, and the poor passengers proportionably alarmed. A remonstrance from them was treated in the usual way.—'And so you want to take the vessel out of my hands—you want to teach me navigation, do you? you ———— picked-up-along-shore numskulls: I'll give you a lesson in navigation before I've done with you.—I've got you in blue water now.'

" The passengers grew warm, which was fortunate, for the cold increased in intensity.

" The mate at last became seriously alarmed for the safety of the ship, particularly when an old whaler, who had the night watch, reported that he could smell icebergs. ' Smell a rope's end!' cried the captain when he was informed of it, ' we are getting into warm latitudes.'   Just then the man on the look out reported icebergs in sight.

" ' There must be some mistake,' cried the captain with an oath; ' come here, mate, let us examine my calculations.' When the skipper again staggered on deck he was laughing uproariously as he shouted, ' What a rum mistake to make! I've been *adding* figures where I should have been *subtracting* them!'   My yarn is ended.   Good night all: only before I go, let me give you a bit of advice, be very careful in the additions you may make.   Good night.   Remember Captain Jock."

A few days after the events just recorded, the usual requisites for forming a station in the bush were gathered together under the practical superintendence of Dodge, who, now he was relieved from the incubus of his difficulties, lent his energies to the new scheme with all the ardour of a boy.

In consequence of Hugh's recent letters bearing intelligence of the gradually declining state of his father's health, he made the necessary arrangements with his partner, and determined to lose no time in visiting England.   Impelled by a sense of duty, not perhaps altogether unalloyed by other inducements, which we may well leave to the reader's imagination, he took advantage of the sailing of the first wool ship, and bade Slinger and his newly acquired friend a hopeful farewell.

They lost no time in stowing their provisions, tools, and other things in a capacious dray, and with a team of eight working bullocks journeyed westward, with many regrets at the absence of their late comrade.   After surmounting the every-day difficulties and tediousness of a bush journey, and passing over the scene of the late fire (the country seemed to be throwing off its

mourning, and appeared once more habited in green), they reached the fine district they had so recently traversed. It presented
many natural advantages for the formation of a future home.
A river of good water flowed through it, and the hills near
were covered with the choicest timber, whilst in one direction
grass-covered plains spread as far as the eye could reach. The
rising ground near the river, which first attracted Dodge's attention on the occasion of the breaking up of the bark canoe,
was eventually fixed upon as the best site on which to erect the
huts.

After months of toil the buildings assumed something like
a habitable appearance, and could our readers have visited the
spot at this time, they might have envied the evident satisfaction and honest pride with which the labourers regarded their
achievements. How delightful was the sleep which visited them
beneath the roof raised by their own right arms!

The weekly day of rest did not pass unheeded, though no
aspiring pinnacles directed the eye heavenward, and no sono-
rous bells echoed through the misty woods proclaiming one spot
more sacred than the rest of earth. They were happy days too,
those Sundays in the far bush, spent in the solitudes of the pri-
meval forest. Under their peaceful influence labors and past
privations were forgotten, and those to come unthought of;
thus the mind was left free to wander where it would. On such
a day, when everything below was bright and lovely, and each
leaf and flower seemed rejoicing in the glorious sunshine, when
the eye instinctively looking upwards pierced through the rich
tracery of boughs and leaves, and resting on

> " the blue sky
> So cloudless, clear, and purely beautiful,
> That God alone was to be seen in Heaven,"

Slinger reclined in front of the hut on some logs arranged so as to form a kind of couch.   He had fallen into a reverie and as the blue wreaths of smoke rose from his pipe sluggishly in the sunshine, they formed the fantastic groundwork on which he built up many a hope for the future.   Happy Slinger! thy airy castles were destined to assume something like reality.

Dodge, who was not given to dream, particularly in broad daylight, had been more practically engaged.   He had been so unfortunate as to break his only pipe, and had nearly completed the construction of another, the only means at his disposal being the bone of a leg of mutton, out of which he had formed the bowl, and the wing bone of a swan serving for a stem. " You seem to like the sunshine," Dodge observed, boring into the mutton bone with his pocket knife.

" I do," Slinger replied, " how bright everything appears!"

" Ah, so it does.   What in the world have you been look- ing so pleased about?   Did you find the tobacco so *very* excel- lent?" Dodge asked, advancing to the fire to turn a pair of shoes he had hung up to dry:—they were sadly deficient of soles, as was rendered palpable by the two forks of the stick on which they depended protruding through the bottoms.

" I've been to England," was Slinger's reply.   " I've look- ed in upon Raymond at home."

" Capital!" Dodge cried smiling, " well, and how did you find him?"

" Dear me," said Slinger, " my mind was engaged on other things, and I forgot to inquire.   Suppose we drink his health in a bumper of tea made extra strong."

" With all my heart," Dodge said, dipping into the tea- chest and casting a handful or two of its contents into the kettle. An economical housekeeper would never have overlooked such extravagance, but then, bushmen and washerwomen know of no moderation in their cups.

"And now," Dodge said, "we must give the station a name. What shall we christen it? You remember how hungry we were when we first came upon it. I like something expressive. What do you think of ' Pinch-gut Slopes!' "

"Oh that won't do," said Slinger. "Supposing Raymond should bring out a wife with him, what a pretty place to date˙ letters from : her English friends would never get through with such an address as that. Try again."

" What do you think of a native name? they are often very musical, and I like the notion of preserving some memento of the tribes who are passing away, leaving nothing to indicate that they ever existed I have heard the natives speak of a river situated about here called ' *Lan-lan-borin.*' Will that do ? "

" Yes, never mind what it means. It is far preferable to such appellations as ' No Good Damper,' ' Wet Jacket Hump,' ' Razor-back Pinch,' and a hundred other such outlandish names." So the station was called Lan-lan-borin.

CHAPTER XV.

IT would be taking an unfair advantage of thee, most patient reader, were we to spin out our story much longer, for is it not clear as the sun at noon day that Hugh Raymond will return with Amy Leslie as his wife, and his father having died, leaving the girls without a protector, what more probable than that they too should accompany their brother, and Slinger's day-dream be realised? As for our eccentric friend Dodge, af-

BB

ter his practical experience had helped to build up the already rising fortunes of the partners, what else, in gratitude, could they do but offer him a share in the station, what more natural than that he should accept it with avidity? But Dodge positively declined the partnership. The reasons he offered were these :—

" You see," he said, " when you amalgamated my cattle, annexed my station, and got me out of the hands of these infernal vampires who were bleeding me slowly to death, you did me a service I can never repay."

" Stuff and nonsense!" Slinger exclaimed.

" Never interrupt a gentleman in his speech," Dodge said with mock solemnity. " Well, I have been able to do you some little good in return, and we are on more equal terms. I perceive great changes are about to take place; for the future I should be only in the way. I shall soon make tracks."

" And if you do," said Slinger with energy, " I'll follow you to the end of creation, I'll upbraid you with ingratitude night and day, and if you go to the jumping-off place I'm after you, mind that. Here's Raymond and I have cut out all our plans, and you want to come in and spoil everything, you ungrateful old creature: give me your hand: we will hear nothing more to the contrary, you *shall* come in as a partner."

" Here's a pretty position for a man to be in," said Dodge; " why how many more partners do you want to take? I hope you don't find " ——— and Dodge whispered the name in Slinger's ear, " so unwilling as I am."

" Hush!" Slinger replied, " its too serious a matter to joke about."

" Don't you make such a mess of it as I did," Dodge continued, unheeding the warning. " I was once in love, a good many years ago though, but you see I have not lost all memory of it, and the lady—I thought her an angel then—appeared to favor my suit. In those days I was not the outlandish looking fellow I am now. I laid out three months' pocket-money on a costly ring and longed for an opportunity to declare my passion. It soon offered, and so did I: with this result. One day, after a *tete-a-tete*, 'Will you favor me, dearest,' said I, seizing her hand, 'by wearing this poor trifle for my sake—will you, in short, consider yourself engaged?' Here I felt myself choking. The lady smiled as she replied, 'Oh, certainly I do.' 'Then permit me,' said I, still retaining the hand I had grasped, but rather taken aback by the easy conquest, 'to imprint one kiss upon those '————'I declare if you do,' said she, all in a pucker, 'I'll tell John.' It turned out that the little minx had been engaged for months to John: I forget his sirname, but as you value my friendship, never christen any of your youngsters John; it has a most hateful sound to me."

Ten years are passed away. Let us visit again the station of Lan-lan-borin. We left it emerging from the surrounding wilderness. Accompany us yet a little further, indulgent reader, and fear not but we will bring thee to our friends in safety. We know their district well: every hill and valley, each watercourse and lagoon, we know their bearings every one; they are as familiar to us as the streets of our native town. Let us hasten towards yonder columns of smoke rising in silvery lines through the trees. Can that comfortable and picturesque homestead be the place we seek? Even so. Industry and energy have overcome all obstacles, and the wilderness " blossoms as the rose." See the surging corn in the spacious paddocks, and the horses and cattle spread over that boundless plain. Come on, we must not loiter now. That peaceful group of cottages, so English in their aspect in all but the luxuriant creepers with which they are netted together, contain within their walls two prosperous and happy families. The garden, common to both, is full of the most lovely flowers such as money could scarcely purchase in England, though here they are in themselves mere weeds. It is the tasteful arrangement of colors which give them all their value. Do you not feel at the first glance that garden was ordered and arranged by woman's hand; that it is to her delicate sensibilities you are indebted for the perfume and the home associations called up by the English honeysuckle creeping round and almost hiding the burly stem of its Australian namesake? The old country is not forgotten. No: no. The tendrils of that fragile plant just strong enough to resist the sea breezes which sweep up the valley, yet form a link in an enduring chain which binds the memory of the exiles to the land of their birth. Let us make for the nearest dwelling. The old kangaroo dog sunning herself on the threshold is quite harmless. Poor Lady's course is well nigh run: grown stiff with scars and age she will dream away the brief existence which remains to her, tended kindly by the hand of the master she has served so long and faithfully. Even her antipathies are forgotten, and alongside her nestles a joey,* one of the pets of the family. "Shoot her!" said Dodge, warmly, to a humane individual who counseled him to kill Lady on the plea that she was quite useless; "Shoot her! I'd sooner stockwhip you."

And has the bushman's life no peculiar attractions to offer? Let us inquire of the parents of that happy group of sunburnt

---

* An infant kangaroo.   When taken young from the mother they are readily tamed

children, whose sports are presided over and shared in by our old friend Dodge, if they have the usual anxieties for the future provision of their offspring? They will tell you their minds are quite easy upon that score, and they doubt not but there will be "room enough for all."

Education, my dear reader! One material branch, at least, is not neglected: early self dependence. See that hardy youngster, who by the likeness we would swear is either a Raymond or a Slinger, we can't exactly say which, trying with all his little might to make an impression upon yon sturdy tree, as he labors determinedly with an axe which might be wielded to greater advantage by a more brawney arm. But the tiny boy is a man in spirit, and the tree, which flourished before his father lived, will fall before him.

There is another youngster; bless us! he has tumbled headlong into the stream which bounds the garden. Fly Dodge, fly to his rescue! Not a bit of it, to swim was one of the first lessons he was taught. Although only eight years old he is well able to save himself. Why that child, Dodge will tell you, was once lost several days in the woods, where he fraternised with a tribe of the aborigines, and when recovered had acquired some proficiency in the art of climbing gum trees for opossums by the aid only of a clumsy stone tomahawk. Save *him* indeed!

Old friends are claiming our attention now. Raymond and Slinger, your hands.—Honest hands too, though horny to the touch and somewhat of the brownest. Dodge, we wish we had a third hand to give you. We are glad to hear the world has gone well with you all: that your business in Melbourne, commenced with a capital of £350, sold for £3,500; that your cattle have multiplied exceedingly under the watchful superintendence of Big Mick, who now resides with his wife and family at the station once owned by Dodge. But above all else we congratulate you on your immunity from the gold fever. The precious metal may be purchased too dearly—the largest nugget grubbed out with the least amount of labor would but ill requite you for the loss of the many comforts and the unalloyed happiness surrounding you in the home you have rescued from the wilderness. Your "pile" is beyond all price.

If shade should result from so much sunshine, may the temperate and healthful lives you lead enable you to do battle with advantage, and to overcome such adverse circumstances as beset men all the world over. So farewell—a long farewell to Lan-lan-borin.

THE END.

W. ROBERTS, PRINTER, 197, HIGH STREET, EXETER.

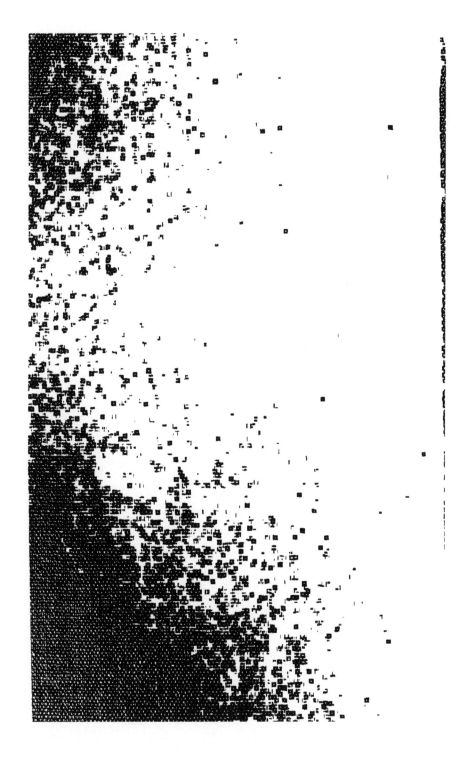

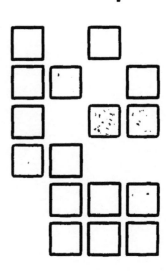

Lightning Source UK Ltd.
Milton Keynes UK
UKHW020643260721
387780UK00009B/1356